REAL MANAGERS

REAL MANAGERS

FRED LUTHANS
RICHARD M. HODGETTS
STUART A. ROSENKRANTZ

BALLINGER PUBLISHING COMPANY
Cambridge, Massachusetts
A Subsidiary of Harper & Row, Publishers, Inc.

International Standard Book Number: 0-88730-103-7

Library of Congress Catalog Card Number: 87-19080

Printed in the United States of America

Library of Congress Cataloging-in-Publication Data

Luthans, Fred.
  Real managers.

  Bibliography: p.
  Includes index.
  1. Management. 2. Executives. I. Hodgetts, Richard M.
II. Rosenkrantz, Stuart A. III. Title.
HD31.L865   1987   658.4   87-19080
ISBN 0-88730-103-7

CONTENTS

List of Figures   ix

List of Tables   xi

Preface   xiii

Chapter 1
A Prologue to Real Managers   1

A Preview of Findings   1
Setting the Stage   2

Chapter 2
What Do Real Managers Do?   5

Previous Studies of Managerial Activites   5
Background of the Real Managers Study   7
Examples of Real Managers' Activities   13
Relative Occurrence of Real Managers' Activities   24
Exploding the Myths of What Managers Do   27

The Confusion Surrounding the Classic Functions
  and Principles   30
The Management Jungle   33

Chapter 3
What Do Successful Real Managers Do?   35

The Lack of Previous Work on Managerial Success   36
Background on the Managerial Success Analysis   36
The Measure of Success Used   37
Activities of Successful Real Managers   38
Most versus Least Successful Real Managers   40
Relative Strengths of the Managerial Activities'
  Relationship to RM Success   41
RM Success Results in Perspective   52
Exploding the Myths of Managerial Success   53

Chapter 4
What Do Effective Real Managers Do?   59

The Traditional Profile of Effective Managers   59
Successful versus Effective Managers   62
How We Defined Managerial Effectiveness   63
Results of the Effectiveness Analysis   66
Exploding the Myths of Managerial Effectiveness   73
A Final Word   75

Chapter 5
Traditional Management Activities   77

The Empirical Backdrop   77
Planning   78
Decisionmaking   84
Controlling   90
A Final Word   93

Chapter 6
Communication Activities   95

The Empirical Backdrop   95
Communication Flows   96
Dealing with Communication Barriers   102

Effective Communication Activities of RMs   107
A Final Word   117

Chapter 7
Networking Activities   119

The Empirical Backdrop   119
The Informal Organization—The Real Organization   121
Power: The Name of the Game   122
Social Skills for Success   125
Political Skills for Success   127
Mentoring: A Specific Networking Strategy   128
The Usefulness of Formal Networks to RMs   129
The Impact of Networks   130
What We Can Learn from Real Managers   132

Chapter 8
Human Resources Management Activities   135

The Empirical Backdrop   135
Motivating and Reinforcing   136
Disciplining and Punishing   143
Managing Conflict   146
Staffing   149
Training and Development   150
A Final Word   155

Chapter 9
Closure and a Point of Departure   157

Summary of Where We Are   157
Successful *and* Effective Real Managers   159
How Our Findings Fit with Modern Management Thinking   162
Management Skills Needed Now and in the Future   173
A Final Word   177

Supplemental Readings and References   179

Index   185

About the Authors   191

LIST OF FIGURES

2-1   Real Manager's Activities   12

2-2   Distribution of Real Managers' Activities   26

2-3   Distribution of Real Managers' Activities,
       Summarized   27

3-1   More versus Less Successful Managers   41

3-2   Relative Contributions to Manager Success   42

4-1   Comparison of the Contributions of RM Activities
       to Effectiveness and Success   67

4-2   Contribution to Manager Effectiveness   68

4-3   Those with Whom RMs Communicate   69

5-1   Distribution of Traditional Management Activities   78

6-1   Distribution of Communication Activities   96

7–1   Distribution of Networking Activities   120

8–1   Distribution of Human Resources Management
       Activities   136

9–1   Determination of Successful *and* Effective RMs   160

9–2   Comparison of Successful *and* Effective Real
       Managers' Activities with the Activities of All
       Real Managers   161

LIST OF TABLES

2-1   The Categories and Behavioral Descriptors
Derived from Free Observation of Forty-four
RMs   10

2-2   Specific Behavioral Incidents of Real Managers'
Activities   14

4-1   Prescriptions for Effective Managers Drawn from
the Literature   60

4-2   Sample Number of Available Measures of Manager
Effectiveness   63

5-1   Traditional Management Activities: Some Examples   79

6-1   Routine Communication Activities: Some Examples   97

6-2   RM Self-reported Communication Flows in Five
Diverse Organizations   98

8–1   Human Resource Management Activities:
Some Examples   138

8–2   "PIGS" Feedback   142

9–1   Concepts and Courses of Action Recommended
in Current Conventional Literature Fit to RM
Activities   172

PREFACE

As the title indicates, this book is about *Real Managers*. And just who are these real managers or, as we refer to them throughout the book, RMs? Importantly, they are not the visible, charismatic leaders of the industrial giants nor even the highly successful executives from the so-called excellent firms. In other words, this book is not about the managers described in the recent best-sellers. Rather, this is the first book that makes an empirical investigation of what mainstream managers from middle-of-the-road organizations really do in their day-to-day activities and how the successful and effective ones do things differently from their unsuccessful and less effective counterparts. In short, this book is about real managers in real organizations—managers with titles such as plant manager, department head, store manager, agency chief, or district manager, from organizations of all sizes in both the private and public sectors.

We gathered data from 457 RMs from numerous organizations in a massive four-year study using multiple methods. The empirical data base from which this book was written was initially gathered from the free observation of 44 RMs in order to determine their managerial activities. Then, trained participant observers systematically gathered data on 248 other RMs in their natural settings. In addition to the free and systematic observation data, we also collected standardized questionnaire data from the RMs' subordinates and intensive interview data of 165 RMs. Chapters 2, 3, and 4 and the supplemental references give the details on samples and analysis techniques used.

As we launched this project, we had to decide whether to do a research monograph, containing numerous footnote references and statistical tables, or a more qualitative and readable presentation that would appeal to a wider audience. Although we did do some articles for academic journals, which are referenced in the back, we opted for a more readable presentation style for this book. However, because we do provide an empirical backdrop to the book, which we feel is a major strength over the popular professional books of recent years, we must present some of the methods and numerical analysis used in the study. The trade-off of our presentation strategy, of course, is that in some instances we do not present enough details to satisfy our academic colleagues interested in such things as reliability coefficients and statistical significance tests; in other instances we may be presenting too much background detail for our practitioner colleagues who want the results and do not want to wade through academic jargon to get there. To reduce the risk of not appealing to either group, we have tried to compromise somewhat, but as a rule of thumb we wrote for the professional manager—the real manager that this book studies. We hope our academic colleagues will use the extended reference section at the end of the book to pursue any unanswered questions or desires for more details on the study.

Very briefly, the study can be summarized in three major phases. In the first phase of the study, we attempted to find an answer to the seemingly obvious, yet intriguing question, "What do managers really do?" The findings in the first phase of our work were used as a point of departure for the more difficult second and third phases. In the second phase, the question of "What do successful managers really do?" was the focus. The third and final phase was aimed at answering perhaps the most important question, "What do effective managers really do?" The answers to these three questions constitute the first half of the book and serve as the empirical backdrop and conceptual framework for the remaining chapters.

There have been considerable interest and concern in recent years about American managers. Once foreign competition, declining productivity, increasing costs, decreasing profits and service, and disgruntled employees finally received the attention of managers across the country, they turned for answers to best-selling books to see how Lee Iacocca manages Chrysler, Harold Geneen managed ITT, and the executives in Peters and Waterman's "excellent" firms do things. Practicing managers obviously found these accounts interesting reading, and, along with Blanchard and Johnson's "one-minute" solutions, they got some good ideas and specific techniques. Now, however, after this first wave of attention, we felt it was time to "flesh out" what was really going on in mainstream organizations and what activities RMs, especially successful and effective ones, do in these organizations.

The book starts from square one. It makes no assumptions about what managers *should* be doing in terms of the traditional prescriptions, or *could* be doing if they were in Lee Iacocca's shoes or worked for one of Peters and Waterman's "excellent" companies. Instead, by undertaking an intensive empirical investigation of what RMs do and what the successful and effective ones do differently than their unsuccessful and less effective counterparts, we dissipated the myths about how practitioners *should* manage to be successful and effective. We went to the best source possible for learning how to be successful and effective— real managers in real organizations, not professors, consultants, writers, or CEOs of the glamour companies.

In particular, this book attempts to replace the myths about the nature of managerial work and how to be successful and effective at it with a data-based systematic analysis. Importantly, we also explore if and what the relationship is between managerial success and managerial effectiveness. The terms "successful" and "effective" are used interchangeably in the management literature. One of the dominant myths surrounding the field of management is that "successful managers" are equated with "effective managers." If RMs are successful, in the sense of being rapidly promoted and/or being the heads of their respective organizations, does that mean they are effective? The answer to this question will become disturbingly clear as the chapters unfold.

The major findings from the investigation of the type of activities of RMs are given specific treatment in separate chapters. Traditional management (Chapter 5), communication (Chapter 6), networking (Chapter 7), and human resources management (Chapter 8), which emerged as being particularly important activities of the RMs, are examined in detail.

In total, the book will aim to restore the confidence of American managers in themselves. We were generally impressed with the RMs we studied; importantly, we demonstrate that they can learn from one another. They don't have to turn to the Japanese or Lee Iacocca or the executives in the "excellent" companies. The major lesson to be learned from this book is that the ways to be successful and effective can be found in real managers themselves.

Because of the size and length of the study upon which this book is based, there were many people who made important contributions along the way. In particular, we would like to recognize and thank Diane Lee Lockwood, Seattle University, for her many ideas and considerable work on the first phase of the study. Also we would like to acknowledge and thank Avis Johnson, University of Akron, and Harry Hennessey, Florida State University, for being part of the research team during the middle phases of the study, and Lew Taylor, University of Miami, in the later phases. Finally, we would like to thank Sang M. Lee, chair of the Department of Management, University of Nebraska, for his administrative support in all aspects of the study and this book. As always, we would like to sincerely thank our wives Kay, Sally, and Polly, for their genuine support and, frankly, for putting up with us over the years.

Fred Luthans
Richard M. Hodgetts
Stuart A. Rosenkrantz

1 A PROLOGUE TO REAL MANAGERS

Management books are flooding the market. For the most part, these books discuss, recommend, and provide guidelines for managers to climb the ladder of success in their organization and effectively manage their people and operations. While this book has a similar objective, unlike all the others, it is based on empirical data about real managers in real organizations. Using participant observation data, supplemented by interviews and questionnaires, we asked what real managers do in their day-to-day activities, what real managers who have been successful in being rapidly promoted in their organizations do, and finally, what real managers who are effective in managing their people and operations do.

A PREVIEW OF FINDINGS

Importantly, we found that the above three questions had surprisingly *different* answers. That is, real managers in the aggregate acted differently from those whom we identified as having experienced relatively rapid promotions in their respective organizations (we call them *successful* real managers) and those whom we identified that had subordinates with relatively high satisfaction and commitment and were judged to have effective organizational units (we call them effective real managers).

1

Of most importance, however, and with potentially profound implications, was our finding that our successful managers were observed to behave quite differently than our effective managers.

This finding—that there is a difference between successful and effective managers—may begin to explain the cause of many of the problems currently facing American organizations. Could it be that the wrong people are being promoted? Could it be that the managers who are effective with their people and their unit's performance are not the ones who are on the fast track? The answers to these and other intriguing questions are the basis of this book.

SETTING THE STAGE

This book, then, presents our real managers, or RMs. On one hand, this is an ambitious undertaking, for RMs do many different things. On the other hand, their activities can fit into an overall framework that allows systematic analysis and evaluation. How RMs traditionally have been portrayed may be accurate in description, but some may be pure conjecture or inference based on a desire to fill in the missing links. In honest retrospect, there have probably been more myths regarding RMs than there have been facts. Nearly all management books to date are prescriptive—they relate what managers *should* do. This book, in contrast, is based on an empirically based description of what they *really do.*

Myths and Realities

There is general agreement that managers get things done through people, but there are questions about how this takes place. Is it a formal process that is preplanned and effectively executed? Or is it a free-flowing type of process that involves a great deal of helter-skelter activity? The traditional view is that management is, or at least *should* be, a rational process. More recently, a small but influential view is that RMs race through their work, often spending no more than a few minutes on each of their varied activities.

In this book we report what we learned from actual observation of RMs in their natural settings. As the chapters unfold, we will lay out a detailed description of what real managers do, what successful real managers do, and what effective real managers do.

Successful versus Effective

At this point, it is important to reiterate that we are making a very clear distinction between *successful* RMs and *effective* RMs. This is confusing, of course, because the two terms are used interchangeably in the management literature and by most of us in our everyday language. Although Chapter 3 on successful RMs and Chapter 4 on effective RMs provide the specific details, we will clarify the distinction at this point because it is a major theme of the book.

Because we made an empirical analysis of RMs, we needed an operational, measurable definition of success and of effectiveness. Thus, we developed measurement indexes of success and effectiveness. It should be noted that these indexes were calculated *after* we had collected the observational data.

The success index was calculated by dividing the RM's level in his or her respective organization (e.g., 1 for the CEO, 4 or 5 for a first-line supervisor depending on how many levels in the given organization) by the tenure in the organization. Using this measure of success, an RM at the fourth level of the organization, who had been there a total of eight years, would be rated more successful than an RM at the third level who had been there for fifteen years. In other words, this empirical measure of success is an index of the speed or velocity of promotion. The derivation, implications, and pro and con arguments surrounding this success measure are discussed in Chapter 3.

Because of the controversy and measurement problems related to the effective performance of managers, this index was even more difficult to determine than the success index. We overcame many of the problems by using a combined measure of effectiveness, which we believed would be more valid than a single dimension. This combined measure consisted of subordinate satisfaction and commitment, and perceived organizational unit performance. The effectiveness index was calculated for the RMs studied. We would have liked to use such "hard measures" as profits and quantity or quality of output or service. However, because we used a large sample of RMs in widely diverse jobs and organizations, we had to depend on standardized questionnaires. The specifics of this measure of effectiveness and the issues surrounding it are discussed in Chapter 4.

For now, we simply want to make a clear, measured distinction between successful RMs and effective RMs. The significance of this distinction will become clear as the chapters unfold.

Theory versus Practice

Besides making the distinctions between myth and reality and between successful and effective, this book illustrates the relationship between theory and practice. Management theory tries to explain why managers act the way they do; management practice describes what managers do. The two approaches, theory and practice, have important but generally ignored linkages. We first describe RMs' activities—what RMs do—then work our way back to why they act this way. The middle part of the book—Chapter 5 "Traditional Activities," Chapter 6 "Communication Activities," Chapter 7 "Networking Activities," and Chapter 8 "Human Resource Management Activities"—exposes the whys and wherefores of RMs. These chapters weave our empirical findings into existing theory and the actual practice of RMs.

Chapter 9 comes full circle, providing closure for our study of RMs and integrating and sorting out what we found. We ask one more important question. What do real managers who are both successful *and* effective do? In addition, we analyze the fit between our findings and existing management theory and practice. The chapter concludes by identifying managerial skills needed now and in the future.

2 WHAT DO REAL MANAGERS DO?

The question posed by the chapter title is not as obvious as it first appears. Many myths surrounding the nature of managerial work have been challenged only recently. We found that when our real managers were observed in their natural, day-to-day work situations, they behaved quite differently than the ways that textbooks, periodicals, common opinion, or even sophisticated research (depending mainly on questionnaire data) have described over the years. This discrepancy—between traditional beliefs about what managers do and what real managers were observed to do—strains the credibility of much that has been written about managers and management. First we will look at previous studies of managerial work, then present the results of our observations of real managers. Finally, we will explode some of the common myths about management.

PREVIOUS STUDIES OF MANAGERIAL ACTIVITIES

Many empirically based studies of leadership and various aspects of management have depended almost solely upon data from standardized questionnaires and interviews. Observational studies of managerial activities, on the other hand, have been very rare. Henry Mintzberg's observational study of five chief executive officers (CEOs) over five-day periods, conducted in the early 1970s has received the most attention.

The Mintzberg Study

Based on detailed observational data, Mintzberg identified five distinguishing characteristics of the managers he studied, and ten "managerial roles." The five characteristics are:

1. Managers work at a relentless pace, seldom taking a break. Upper level managers often take their work home. Most are obsessive about their jobs.
2. Managers typically spend brief amounts of time on fragmented activities, and are frequently interrupted. These characteristics are more pronounced at lower management levels.
3. Managers tend to direct their attention to concrete issues and to the most current information, rather than to reflective planning.
4. Managers spend one-third of their total time communicating with outsiders and a third to a half of their time communicating with subordinates.
5. Managers conduct two-thirds of their communications orally, mostly by telephone or at unscheduled meetings.

Mintzberg's study was pioneering in that he used observational methods and, more importantly, that his findings generally contradict traditional beliefs, as well as the body of literature about what managers do or should do.

Of equal interest are the following often cited ten roles identified by Mintzberg:

1. Figurehead—doing ritual, ceremonial or symbolic tasks;
2. Leader—guiding, hiring, firing, training, praising, promoting and evaluating;
3. Liaison—maintaining connections outside the work unit;
4. Monitor—keeping abreast of information;
5. Disseminator—passing information to subordinates;
6. Spokesperson—representing work unit interests to upper level management;
7. Entrepreneur—initiating controlled change in the work unit;
8. Disturbance Handler—handling crises;

9. Resources Allocator—controlling money, employees, material, equipment, facilities and services; and
10. Negotiator—committing organizational resources to and from the work unit; this can apply to unions, contracts, other organizations.

The Kotter Study

Besides the Mintzberg study, there have been only a few other observational studies of managerial work. The most prominent and recent was a study of fifteen general managers by Harvard Professor John Kotter conducted in the early 1980s. Supplementing many hours of observation with questionnaires and interviews, Kotter found the following six job demands on the managers studied:

1. Setting basic goals and policies in an uncertain environment;
2. Balancing the allocation of scarce resources among a wide range of users while protecting long-term goals;
3. Monitoring and controlling complex activities, recognizing and extinguishing "fires" quickly;
4. Getting information, cooperation and support from upper level management to do the job; demanding support without alienating upper level managers;
5. Getting cooperation from corporate staff, unions and big customers to overcome resistance, red tape and other obstacles; and
6. Motivating subordinates and controlling unacceptable performance and interdepartmental conflicts.

When Kotter's job demands are compared to Mintzberg's roles, we find that many of them are similar. However, overall, Kotter stresses that his general managers have two common activities—agenda-setting and networking. Agenda-setting appears to be a type of "reflective planning" that Mintzberg said managers don't do, and the networking is similar to informal politicking, an area that Mintzberg did not address directly.

BACKGROUND OF THE REAL MANAGERS STUDY

Our study of real managers took place over a four-year period. Unlike the Mintzberg or Kotter studies, we did not limit ourselves to a small sample of elite managers; instead, we gathered data on literally hundreds of managers from numerous diverse organizations. Also unlike the multitude of previous studies in the fields of organizational behavior and human resource management, we did not depend on a single method to gather the data. We used both free observation and systematic participant observation in the natural setting, supplemented by intensive interviews and standardized questionnaires. We carefully analyzed the data throughout the study to monitor its reliability and validity. For the interested reader, the supplemental readings and references listed at the back of the book cite various journal articles that describe in detail the various aspects (sample sizes, reliabilities, validity analysis, etc.) of the study.

Unstructured, Free Observation of Real Managers

To answer the question "What do real managers do?", we first used trained observers to freely observe and carefully record all the behaviors and activities of forty-four real managers in their natural setting. These real managers held bona fide managerial positions; all had people working directly for them. They came from all levels (lower, middle, and upper) and all types of organizations (e.g., manufacturing plants, retail stores, hospitals, corporate headquarters, a railroad, government agencies, insurance companies, a newspaper office, and financial institutions).

The real managers in this first phase of the study were observed in a completely unstructured format for a varied hour each day over a two-week period (i.e., 440 hours of unstructured observation of RMs in their current, natural situations). The forty-four observers in this first phase of the study participated in an extensive training workshop that emphasized the systematic errors commonly found in observing others. By writing observation logs from several role-playing exercises that we critiqued, the trainees learned how to observe the behavior of the target RM continuously over an hour and to record specific, identifiable behaviors and activities on their logs. They were taught to be reporters concentrating on objective description rather than evaluating the behaviors and activities observed.

The observers systematically varied their hours throughout each working day during the two weeks to assure representativeness. After the two weeks, the forty-four RMs were shown copies of the logs on their behaviors and activities and were asked to rate to what extent these were typical of their day-to-day behavior and activities. On a scale of 1 to 5, the average was a 4, indicating that these descriptions were typical "to a considerable extent." All data from this first unstructured observation phase were only a prelude to establishing the categories for our observation system used to gather data for the major, subsequent phases of the study.

Reducing the Free Observation Data into Categories of Managerial Activities

After gathering data from the free observation of the forty-four RMs, we faced the considerable task of reducing it to workable categories of managerial activities. To do this, we used the Delphi process, first developed and used during the heyday of Rand Corporation's "Think Tank" in the 1950s. The Delphi process consists of using members of a panel to make independent, autonomous judgments. These judgments are then summarized and fed back to the panel members. The panel members, using the composite feedback, then make further anonymous judgments. Our Delphi panel consisted of seven members, four from the research team and three relatively naive (unbiased) members who were selected specifically because they had no prior knowledge of the management literature or practical management experience. We gave this panel instructions on the Delphi process and required the members to read and become familiar with handouts describing the construction of adequate behavioral categories from raw data.

In the first Delphi round, the panel members independently reviewed the extensive logs completed by the forty-four observers, and autonomously suggested about 100 general categories of managerial activity with accompanying behavioral descriptors. These categories were fed back to the panelists with accompanying anonymous comments. Through several iterations, the panelists continued to reduce the categories into smaller but more comprehensive sets. Table 2–1 shows the final twelve categories and the accompanying behavioral descriptors.

The categories in Table 2–1 not only are representative of the free observation data on the forty-four RMs initially studied, but also are quite comprehensive, use generally recognized terminology, and are mutually exclusive. However, for ease of presentation and to synthesize the activities of real managers, we collapse the twelve categories into

Table 2-1. The Categories and Behavioral Descriptors Derived from Free Observation of Forty-four RMs.[a]

1. Planning
   - setting goals and objectives
   - defining tasks needed to accomplish goals
   - scheduling employees, timetables
   - assigning tasks and providing routine instructions
   - coordinating activities of different subordinates to keep work running smoothly
   - organizing the work

2. Staffing
   - developing job descriptions for position openings
   - reviewing applications
   - interviewing applicants
   - hiring
   - contacting applicants to inform them of hiring decision
   - "filling in" where needed

3. Training/Developing
   - orienting employees, arranging for training seminars, etc.
   - clarifying roles, duties, job descriptions
   - coaching, mentoring, walking subordinates through task
   - helping subordinate with personal development plans

7. Controlling
   - inspecting work
   - walking around
   - monitoring performance data (e.g., computer printouts, production, financial reports)
   - practicing preventive maintenance

8. Motivating/Reinforcing
   - allocating formal organizational rewards
   - asking for input, participation
   - conveying appreciation, compliments
   - giving credit where due
   - listening to suggestions
   - giving positive performance feedback
   - increasing job challenge
   - delegating responsibility and authority
   - letting subordinates determine how to do their own work
   - supporting the group before superiors and others, backing a subordinate

9. Disciplining/Punishing
   - enforcing rules and policies
   - glaring, nonverbal harassing
   - demoting, firing, laying off employee
   - issuing any formal organizational reprimand or notice

4. Decisionmaking
   - defining problems
   - choosing between two or more alternatives or strategies
   - handling day-to-day operational crises as they arise
   - weighing the tradeoffs; cost/benefit analysis
   - making the decision
   - developing new procedures to increase efficiency
5. Handling Paperwork
   - processing mail
   - reading reports, in-box
   - writing reports, memos, letters, etc.
   - doing routine financial reporting and bookkeeping
   - doing general desk work
6. Exchanging Information
   - answering routine procedural questions
   - receiving and disseminating requested information
   - conveying results of meetings
   - giving or receiving routine information over the phone
   - holding staff meetings of an informational nature (e.g., status updates, new company policies, etc.)

   - ''chewing out'' a subordinate, criticizing
   - giving negative performance feedback

10. Interacting with Others
    - public relations
    - contacts with customers
    - contacts with suppliers, vendors
    - external meetings
    - community service activities
11. Managing Conflict
    - managing interpersonal conflict between subordinates or others
    - appealing to higher authority to resolve a dispute
    - appealing to third-party negotiators
    - seeking cooperation or consensus between conflicting parties
    - attempting to resolve conflicts between subordinate and self
12. Socializing/Politicking
    - engaging in nonwork-related chitchat (e.g., family or personal matters)
    - ''joking around''
    - discussing rumors, hearsay, grapevine
    - complaining, griping, downgrading others
    - politicking, gamesmanship

---

[a]Adapted from Fred Luthans and Diane Lockwood, ''Toward an Observation System for Measuring Leader Behavior in Natural Settings,'' in J.G. Hunt, D. Hosking, C. Schriesheim, and R. Stewart, eds., *Leaders and Managers* (New York: Pergamon, 1984), p. 122. This article makes a detailed statistical assessment of the reliability and validity of these categories of leader behavior.

the four comprehensive activities shown in Figure 2–1. Thus, our initial answer to the question of "What do real managers do?" is: (1) communication activities; (2) traditional management activities; (3) networking activities; and (4) human resource management activities. Importantly, these are the empirically derived activities of real managers as opposed to the "armchair"-derived normative functions of managers portrayed in the management literature over the years.

Follow-up Interviews

The managerial activities identified in Table 2–1 and Figure 2–1 provided a foundation and point of departure for our study of real managers. However, to provide follow-up and to get more intensive descriptions of and qualitative data on these activities, we next conducted 165 interviews of a completely different set of real managers. Like the first set of 44,

Figure 2–1. Real Managers' Activities (*N* = 44 RMs using free-observation data).

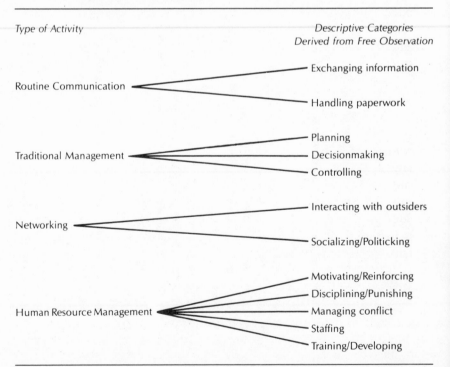

Type of Activity	Descriptive Categories Derived from Free Observation
Routine Communication	Exchanging information / Handling paperwork
Traditional Management	Planning / Decisionmaking / Controlling
Networking	Interacting with outsiders / Socializing/Politicking
Human Resource Management	Motivating/Reinforcing / Disciplining/Punishing / Managing conflict / Staffing / Training/Developing

these 165 RMs were from all levels and all types of organizations. The trained interviewers first asked subordinates for examples of their immediate boss's behavior for each of the twelve categories of managerial work.

The interviewers asked for a specific incident that represented a great, an average, and a low amount of the given activity. Using a systematic retranslation method to sort these incidents, a team of researchers and practicing RMs reduced the incidents to those most representative of the categories. Table 2–2 summarizes these representative, real incidents for each category. In combination, the free observation of the 44 RMs and interviews from subordinates about the 165 RMs provide a comprehensive and, we believe, most accurate picture of what managers really do.

EXAMPLES OF REAL MANAGERS' ACTIVITIES

Table 2–1 lists the directly observable behavioral descriptors derived from our study and Table 2–2 the specific behavioral incidents that emerged from the interviewing portion of the study. However, to gain further insights, we needed to hear from RMs themselves and their subordinates and colleagues (rather than just researchers, including ourselves, or textbook writers) exactly what is involved in these activities. Here are some examples (not necessarily direct quotes) of each category garnered from our interactions with real managers over the course of the study.

Communication Activities

Exchanging Information
Manager: Because I'm on the road so much, I have a scheduled meeting with my people every Monday morning. We rarely have an agenda. It's a discussion meeting to exchange information about our products and to share new methods and procedures that I have picked up on my trips. It's as informal as possible to keep communications open. Everyone participates; no one preaches.

Subordinate: He sometimes uses a very formal approach, for example, posting a memo to be initialed by each person in each department. Then he follows it up with a discussion at monthly department meetings. To help him keep abreast of things, he sometimes convenes an on-the-spot meeting with the department heads.

Table 2-2. Specific Behavioral Incidents of Real Managers' Activities ($N = 165$, drawn from structured interviews).

Type of Activity	Descriptive Category	Amount	Behavioral Incident Derived from Interviews
Communication			
	Exchanging Routine Information	High	Every week has a scheduled meeting with subordinates, shares ideas and leads a discussion about new methods and procedures.
			After meeting with other managers, distributes the meeting's notes to subordinates.
		Medium	Learns of a change, walks into the general office or work area, and announces it.
			Holds a monthly meeting to pass on data received at staff meetings attended with other managers.
		Low	Posts notices on bulletin board for employees to read.
			Circulates an interoffice memo with no requests for response or feedback.
	Handling Paperwork	High	Prepares daily, weekly, and monthly reports, which include costs reports and comparisons with past records and activities.
			Pays bills, submits orders, completes payroll checks, and compares cash receipts or similar data.
		Medium	Records figures from work units several times a day and records the totals at the end of the day.
			Reads the daily mail and routes it to employees.
		Low	Checks correspondence, such as incoming mail and advertising.
			Signs attendance reports.

Traditional Management

Planning	High	Sets goals and then holds face-to-face meetings with workers, giving specific instructions, review dates, and deadlines.
		Reviews past budgets, operations data, and expense figures, consults with other departments, and then sets specific goals for the next year.
	Medium	Develops a work schedule for a given project.
		Assigns employees for different jobs and time schedules.
	Low	Budgets time between departments or work areas.
		Assigns employees the materials, tools, and equipment they are to use for the day.
Decision-making	High	Reads all facts related to the problem or issue and discusses the facts with others involved. Considers short- and long-term impacts, makes recommendations to higher management, and implements final decisions.
		Makes a judgment on a major acquisition, an important policy change, or a new service or product.
	Medium	Notices a problem, discusses it with another supervisor or with specialists in the area, and then selects a course of action.
		Delegates the problem to someone closer to the situation and then receives a follow-up report or phone call on the solution.
	Low	Delegates or refers minor problems or situations to the next person in line.
		Reviews the situation and tells a subordinate, "You'll have to handle it."

Table 2-2. (continued)

Type of Activity	Descriptive Category	Amount	Behavioral Incident Derived from Interviews
Traditional Management (continued)	Controlling	High	Makes personal visits to work areas in different departments or units on a scheduled basis to check work progress and compares summaries or employees' performance to standards.
			Reviews the time already spent and the time remaining on projects and meets with employees to control efficiency problems.
		Medium	Checks to see how long it took to do a job and to inspect finished products or services.
			Reviews reports and performance of routine functions to ensure they are running smoothly and goes over reports with employees.
		Low	Telephones to check on operations.
			Tours the office to see if people are working and to check on equipment.
Networking	Interacting with Outsiders	High	Seeks involvement in public relations activities, such as attending community events.
			Handles customer/client relations with other organizations in the industry and meets with members of clubs important to the organization.
		Medium	Gives presentations at service clubs or similar organizations.
			Has lunch with suppliers of materials to discuss how things are

	Low	Takes phone calls from suppliers.
		Talks with customers/clients who ask about a product or service.
Socializing/ Politicking	High	Entertains top-level managers in the organization, such as playing tennis or going fishing with them.
		Keeps an active social calendar and possibly holds an open house with food and drink for employees.
	Medium	Socializes with the employees before a staff meeting begins.
		Socializes with employees in the lounge or gathering place.
	Low	Talks with peers and subordinates in the cafeteria or gathering place during lunch.
		Has a cup of coffee with the staff.
Human Resource Management		
Motivating/ Reinforcing	High	Immediately compliments a subordinate who handles an irate customer/client very well.
		Sends a letter of praise to an employee who has done an excellent job.
	Medium	Compliments an employee before co-workers at a staff meeting or in the presence of other managers.
		Has individual discussions with subordinates to compliment them on work they have done well.
	Low	Says to an employee, "Now that is really good," and puts a hand on the employee's shoulder.
		Tells an employee in passing, that he or she had a good week or did a good job on some task.

Table 2-2. (continued)

Type of Activity	Descriptive Category	Amount	Behavioral Incident Derived from Interviews
Human Resource Management (continued)	Disciplining/ Punishing	High	Suspends an employee without pay for unsatisfactory performance. Writes a reprimand, sends copies to the employee and the personnel file, and uses this information in determining the employee's annual wage increase.
		Medium	Places an employee on probation for recurrent lateness. Writes a formal notice of undesirable actions by an employee, gives a copy to the employee, and puts one in the personnel file.
		Low	Reprimands an employee for occasional lateness or for a performance problem. Raises her or his voice at an employee for making a long distance phone call and not recording it.
	Managing Conflict	High	Explains the reasons for decision to co-workers upset because one worker received a promotion. Talks face-to-face with two employees whose functions overlap when one of them believes the other receives too much recognition or salary, listens to both, and sorts out the facts.
		Medium	Personally talks to subordinates who are not getting along. Mediates when two subordinates are having a disagreement about the date when a new procedure should start.
		Low	Separates employees to avoid further argument.

Staffing	High	When filling a position, considers in-house personnel for promotion, reviews outside applications, holds interviews, reviews information, and makes the selection decision.
		Designs job descriptions, screens applications, interviews applicants, and selects the new employees.
	Medium	Sets wages and benefits for a new employee, after the hiring decision is made.
		Checks past work experience of applicants who appear to be acceptable.
	Low	Makes the decision to hire a new employee or interviews the new employee on the first day of work.
		Goes outside of company to find replacements who meet certain criteria.
Training Developing	High	Brings in experts and films and arranges programs for employees.
		Coaches the staff on necessary work processes, organizes presentations of procedures through slides and transparencies, and involves the staff in practical training exercises.
	Medium	Conducts in-house meetings to review specific techniques or procedures.
		Teaches the more difficult jobs, such as operating the equipment or tasks which require coordination with other workers, to certain employees.
	Low	Gives subordinates job descriptions and written procedures from which to learn their responsibilities.

Handling Paperwork
Subordinate: The paperwork he does consists of reading reports, reading other people's work, and reading informational material. He's developed a routine so that he can read his mail and answer as much as he can, first thing every morning, by closing the door, minimizing his contact with other people. He has his phone answered and uses the dictaphone. He's really energetic and moves like an athlete during this time.

Colleague: When he's doing his paperwork, he really seems relaxed. He leaves the door open, moves slowly, and seems to enjoy and encourage interruptions. I don't think that he behaves the way he does because he enjoys the paperwork. I think he tries to escape from it. If anyone in this company meticulously read everything on his desk, and organized the hell out of it, he'd be here until midnight every night. He'd be a full-time clerk, with no time to manage well. One-third gets delegated, one-third gets resolved, and one-third (probably informational) goes in the trash can.

Traditional Management Activities

Planning
Manager: As we put together the objectives for this year, I consider a lot of ideas and projects—where they fit best, what are the political implications. We have to reject inappropriate proposals, create new objectives, and integrate everything into a long-range corporate plan. Because my company has a fast growth rate, we have an unstructured planning process—we have to be on our toes to make sure that no one is left out and nothing important is overlooked.

Manager: I usually gather my group togther and they inform me of the issues we'll have to deal with during the next few months. I schedule weekly meetings, with a published agenda, and I encourage my people to create do-able solutions. I also keep in touch with the corporate staff and with the people in other departments who I know have the best information in that particular area.

Decisionmaking
Manager: I had a major disagreement with the treasurer about formal presentations at our executive meetings. As I probed for reasons behind

the disagreement, we recognized the underlying factors and our feelings about the issue. This enabled me to combine the strengths of both our positions into a joint solution.

Subordinate: She often, but not always, seems to arrive at a decision through consensus. Sometimes she lists problems and possible solutions with costs and benefits for each one. When she's problemsolving, she consults with good resource people and with other managers. She checks any relevant literature she can find, considers the problem for awhile, and makes her own decision.

Controlling

Subordinate: He monitors the progress of systems development projects. He reviews these at weekly meetings and wants to know about deviations from schedule, delays, and major problems. He also has a printout for each activity that he uses to compare the performances of his lower level managers. If performance is low, he finds out why, then makes a decison about whether to intervene.

Subordinate: He doesn't monitor in a way that makes me gun-shy. He monitors the critical things closely but he doesn't stifle me. He expects me to do my job and to tell him when my subordinates are doing well. He often tells me about a problem, gives me some insight into it, and leaves me to solve it. He always follows up later to see how I've done.

Networking Activities

Interacting with Outsiders

Subordinate: He is always on the telephone, keeping contacts with other managers, with customers, and with suppliers. When he isn't on the job at the plant, he's out developing contacts in the community or attending some meeting.

Colleague: She is always out getting volunteer workers or volunteer speakers. I used to worry about her becoming too involved in community affairs, but she seems to be able to select those people who are likely to support us.

Socializing/Politicking
Subordinate: He often has lunch with managers one and two levels above him. The conversations at those luncheons usually revolve around social issues and about what is going on in the department. He's greased the skids for me more than once. I owe him a lot.

Colleague: He's got a lot of clout. He socializes with the powerful personalities in the company and with prominent community leaders outside the company. His position in the company isn't very high, but he seems to have formidable influence everywhere. I would hate to think of him as anything but a good friend when I need to get something done.

Human Resources Management Activities

Motivating/Reinforcing
Subordinate: He tells me when I'm doing well, and he tells higher level management when I'm doing well. I know this because they come to me to congratulate me for good progress on a given project. He even remembers birthdays and holidays. He's got an informal incentive program where the best performer for the month is designated "star of the month" and is invited to a free lunch.

Subordinate: She's highly motivated herself, and it's infectious. Whenever an Emergency Code is well run on the floor and the doctors are complimentary, she always lets us know how pleased they are with us. What a contrast to her predecessor! She provided *no* feedback, had no incentive programs, and never praised anyone for a job well done.

Disciplining/Punishing
Colleague: He fired a person on the spot for harassing another individual. He doesn't hesitate to give verbal reprimands. When he cannot tolerate continued activity or inactivity of any particular kind, he leaves no doubt about what he expects.

Subordinate: Before he fired him, he brought the subordinate to his office, told him what he was doing wrong and how he wanted it done, and then gave him a chance to do it correctly. When the subordinate continued to do it wrong, he replaced him.

Managing Conflict
Colleague: There was a performance problem due to a conflict between him and another manager. At first, there really wasn't any attempt to resolve it. Finally, the manager just told the other guy that he was right and that was that. He admitted he was wrong and things now run more smoothly.

Subordinate: He often manages conflict by anticipating and preventing it. He usually gets the potentially conflicting parties together and arrives at a joint solution before open conflict really erupts.

Staffing
Manager: When I hired an attorney for the company, it was a very long, involved, and careful process. Our executive committee listed the attorney's duties and I designed a profile. We contract with a selection firm that recruits, tests, and pre-screens salaried employees for us. When this company found likely candidates, I flew to other cities to interview them and narrowed the field to four. Then I invited them to the home office to interview with the rest of the staff.

Manager: I have to find candidates for openings, by advertising and by word-of-mouth. I always have to check the most current Equal Employment Opportunity regulations to keep out of trouble. I'm constantly planning for future personnel moves and trying to replace people we lose with little or no notice. Recruiting and hiring people to get the work done around here is a continuing challenge.

Training/Developing
Subordinate: The boss has been known to stop employees on the production line to demonstrate a correct procedure. He hasn't had any formal training for managing at this level, so he gets tips and suggestions and reads articles that Jack gives him. He's great at developing his subordinates. He sends clippings, makes telephone calls, gives tips, and often tells them about better ways to do things. He also tries to have his supervisory people attend as many motivational conferences and seminars as he can.

Manager: We don't have formal training here. When I started, I received no training. Each of us was turned loose and we were expected to train ourselves. I expected some kind of formal orientation as a minimum for training, but even that wasn't provided. It's strange, because the boss says that formal training is an unnecessary expense to the company, but he spends a lot of his own time developing the people around him.

Combined with the unstructured observation and the interviews obtaining specific incidents, these representative examples provide a comprehensive, multiple-measure empirical basis for answering the question of what real managers do.

RELATIVE OCCURRENCE OF REAL MANAGERS' ACTIVITIES

Once we were satisfied that the free, unstructured observation of 44 RMs in their natural settings, the interviews about 165 other RMs, and the representative incidents provided an accurate answer to what real managers do, we turned our attention to the relative occurrence of the activities. We used another set of data to analyze the relative frequencies of the real managers' activities. Specifically, three waves (three points in time, each about a year apart) of structured observational data on 248 RMs from all levels and types of organizations were aggregated. To gather these data, trained participant observers filled out a managerial activities checklist, based on Table 2–1, eighty times over a two-week period. These observations took place during a predetermined, random ten-minute period of each working hour.

Training of Participant Observers

The participant observers were selected on the basis of their having maximum visual and audible contact with the target RM and their understanding of the functions, terminology, and nature of the work performed by the target RM.

Each of the observers participated in an extensive training workshop conducted by the researchers. The first half of the training provided the following:

1.   A general explanation of the purpose of the observations, in which the observers were told that the data would not only assist the research but would also be used for executive development purposes, and that the observers' findings would always be kept anonymous;

2. A discussion of the observation form, with special attention to defining and interpreting the behavioral categories;
3. Careful instruction on how to overcome potential observation errors; and
4. Instructions to be as unobtrusive as possible when recording behaviors and to keep the targeted RMs unaware of the nature of the behavioral categories noted or when they would be observed.

Because we used *participant* observers who were in constant contact with the targeted RMs, intrusiveness in recording the behaviors was minimized.

The second half of the training was devoted to modeling and actual practice through role playing. To evaluate the training, an elaborate skit that included six predetermined managerial activities was presented to the trainees. The trained participant observers' responses in this evaluation had an overall mean accuracy of 92.5 percent.

Because our trained participant observers generally were unable to observe the disciplining/punishing activity directly, we deleted this activity from later study and from our analysis of the relative frequencies of the managerial activities. We know from our interview data that this activity is done, but (mercifully) our observers were generally unable to record it. The inference to be drawn here is that most disciplining/punishing is done rarely and in private.

Distribution of Real Manager's Activities

How RMs divide their time and effort among the eleven descriptive managerial activities is shown in Figure 2–2. The pie chart displays average frequencies for the observed 248 RMs at all levels. However, further analysis revealed that some activities are sensitive to the level of the RM. For example, bottom–level real managers have the least opportunity to do the traditional management activity of planning or the networking activity of interacting with outsiders. We'll examine some of these differences between top-, middle-, and first-level managers in more detail in Chapter 3.

As shown in Figure 2–2, real managers spend almost a third of their time and effort in communications activities (exchanging information and handling paperwork). Another third is spent in the traditional management activities (planning, decisionmaking, and controlling). That leaves about a fifth of their time and effort for networking activities

Figure 2-2. Distribution of Real Managers' Activities (*N* = 248 RMs drawn from participant observation data).

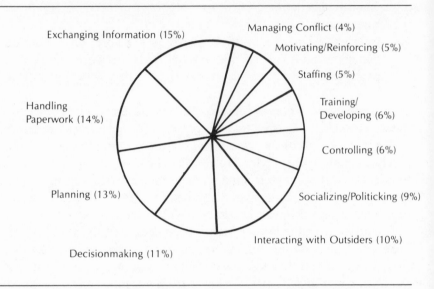

Exchanging Information (15%)

Managing Conflict (4%)

Motivating/Reinforcing (5%)

Staffing (5%)

Handling Paperwork (14%)

Training/ Developing (6%)

Controlling (6%)

Planning (13%)

Socializing/Politicking (9%)

Interacting with Outsiders (10%)

Decisionmaking (11%)

(interacting with outsiders and socializing/politicking) and a fifth for human resource management activities (motivating/reinforcing, staffing, training/developing and managing conflict). Figure 2–3 shows the relative distribution of these four aggregated activities, providing a more definitive answer to the question, "What do real managers do?".

RM Results in Perspective

In agreement with conventional wisdom about managers, Figure 2–3 shows that RMs do spend a lot of their time in routine communication and traditional management activities. However, this conflicts somewhat with both Mintzberg's and Kotter's findings. For example, Mintzberg concluded that his CEOs did not do planning (as defined by his criteria), and Kotter concluded that his general managers really did little decisionmaking (as defined by his criteria). Contrary to common notions, however, we found that real managers devote a relatively great amount of their efforts to human resource management and networking activities, which have been virtually ignored in the traditional management literature. One exception is Kotter, who does include the networking

Figure 2-3. Distribution of Real Manager Activities, Summarized (*N* = 248 RMs drawn from participant observation data).

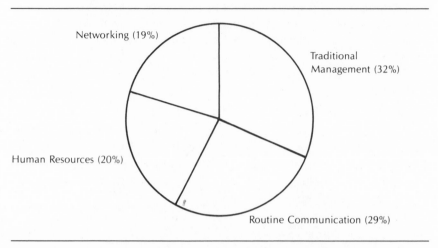

Networking (19%)

Traditional Management (32%)

Human Resources (20%)

Routine Communication (29%)

activity in his discussion of general managers. The behaviorally oriented literature, of course, focuses on human resource management activities.

EXPLODING THE MYTHS OF WHAT MANAGERS DO

The discrepancy between commonly held beliefs and expectations about what managers *should* be doing, what academics *think* they're doing, and what they *really* do was disturbing even to some of the real managers themselves. One real manager elaborated:

> We all went through the B-schools when we were young and the professors had all the answers on the blackboards, computer printouts, and reading assignments. Everything was so clean and precise. The problems in the accounting and quantitative courses always had logical answers. Even the principles of management and policy courses had structure and form, citing the five functions a manager performs or the three steps of strategic planning. The same is true of the management development programs I have attended over the years. The trainer has all the answers to my problems—one, two, three. But I'm here to tell you it really isn't like that. My day consists of running from one meeting to the next, fielding questions from my internal staff and outsiders, trying to respond to telephone messages, trying

to smooth over an argument between a couple of people, and keeping my ever higher in-basket from toppling down on top of me. In fact, I feel guilty that I'm not doing the things that the management educators, trainers, and the things I read say that I *should* be doing. When I come out of one of these sessions, or after reading the latest management treatise, I'm eager and ready to do it. Then the first phone call from an irate customer, or a new project with a rush deadline, falls on me, and I'm back in the same old rut. I don't have time for time management, let alone strategic planning and designing a matrix structure for my unit.

Real managers have been faced with this dilemma for years. They say to themselves, "The book/professor/trainer says one thing, but I'm doing something else. I must be wrong, because what I'm doing has little or nothing to do with what they are talking about." What the books, professors, and trainers are talking about may be just myths surrounding the nature of managerial work.

Myth No. 1: Managers Do Reflective, Strategic Planning.   One assumption has been that all managers systematically receive information that enables them to anticipate future developments in time to adapt to expected needs in some orderly manner. In other words, they do reflective, strategic planning. Mintzberg discounted this altogether. We found that real managers do some planning (see Figure 2–2), but not necessarily in the sophisticated ways portrayed in the strategic management literature. More realistically, higher level managers may proceed with caution and plain old-fashioned fear, both natural and appropriate reactions, when making decisions. This process is not what the textbooks describe as strategic planning, but the practical result is in some ways similar. Decisions are deferred or delayed until as much information as possible is gathered at the higher levels. Unfortunately, however, the more time taken for decisionmaking at the top, the less time is available for mid-level and lower managers to plan and to act. This makes the RMs' jobs more chaotic and it limits their planning to a short-run, or even an immediate, reactive, tactical approach, rather than a reflective, strategic approach.

Myth No. 2: Managers Organize with Formal Structures and Procedures.   Managers are commonly believed to organize by designing formal authority/responsibility structures. Yet, in real organizations, formalizing all structures and procedures is likely to be discouraged, if not prohibited. In most organizations, paper is already the "most important product." As shown in Figure 2–2, we found paperwork one of the most dominant activities of real managers. Importantly, however, we found that real managers deliberately avoid paperwork, which goes hand-in-hand with formalized structures and the accompanying written policies and procedures. Additionally, top-level centralized control aborts any attempt by mid- or lower level managers to implement their own authority/responsibility structures. Instead, organizing is often done through meetings and on the basis of personality and style (i.e., the networking activity of RMs) rather than through formalized structures and procedures.

Myth No. 3: Managers Do Systematic, Proactive Staffing. The traditional approach to the staffing function of management is to anticipate and plan proactively for future personnel and training needs in a manager's area of responsibility. Then managers proceed to select, train, and evaluate their people, that is, they perform a proactive staffing function. As Figure 2–2 shows, real managers do relatively little of this staffing activity. We found that unless RMs were part of long-range planning to create or to phase down their operations, they had little warning of future staffing needs. More often than not, their people left on very short notice, due to accidents, health, or personal reasons. One manager explained:

> This notion of proactive, human resource planning is ridiculous. Over the thirteen years I have been in charge of this department, I have had my share of turnover, but very little of it I could anticipate or plan for. Sure, I know about contingency planning and probability estimates. But I still maintain that it makes no sense in predicting who quits and who doesn't, or how many will quit in a given period of time. I just have to react to the personal whims of my people as they come and go.

Very few organizations maintain a pipeline of suitable hiring candidates. Typical search periods of two to twenty weeks, or even longer, are not uncommon when trying to replace employees. Real managers have to face this problem constantly; the training/developing aspect of human resource management becomes an eternal struggle to survive, with the immediate goal of simply maintaining current productivity, let alone improving it. The appraisal aspect of the staffing function may become a bureaucratic requirement to fill out some subjective forms once or, at most, twice a year.

Myth No. 4: Managers Operate under Well-defined Chains of Command. Traditional management assumes that unity of command prevails. Each manager reports to only one boss in the chain of command. Yet, as one manager described, this assumption may not be valid:

During the course of a single day, I am interrupted and diverted from what I'm doing on an almost continual basis. When I plan my day, the list of to-dos helps keep me from getting lost among the interruptions. But I'm a results-oriented manager, and it's frustrating to see the amount of work that I'm not getting done. Upper level management acts as if they're still operating at my level. Why can't they grow into the level to which they've been promoted? I've counted at least a dozen people who tell me to drop whatever I'm doing to go to an unscheduled meeting, or to do something I don't want to do or really *shouldn't* do, in order to do my job properly.

The managers making peremptory demands on others sincerely believe that their requirements are a justifiable exception in the chain of command. Here again, we found that real managers are coping creatively with a problem that traditional theory tells us should not exist.

Myth No. 5: Traditional Principles Simplify Managing. The traditional principles, designed to simplify the managerial process, may be delivering less than promised. Although we definitely found RMs doing them (see Figures 2–2 and 2–3), their greatest contribution may be simply to provide us with a common managerial vocabulary. As in holy writ, there is a traditional management principle for what RMs *should* do that can be interpreted for every possible management situation. Some of these principles are confusing at best and contradictory at worst.

As we examined them in detail, the imperfections became painfully clear. A review of some of these principles will point out the difficulty, if not the impossibility, that RMs have in reconciling them in any given situation.

THE CONFUSION SURROUNDING THE CLASSIC FUNCTIONS AND PRINCIPLES

The pioneering management theorist Henri Fayol identified five functions of management: planning, organizing, commanding, coordinating, and controlling. Management texts still teach these five functions, in one form or another, and beginning management students are duly impressed. "Here are the five things that you, as a manager, must do to win the game—to be effective," the texts declare. No wonder real managers are frustrated about the lack of such "clean" solutions in their fuzzy, "unclean" real world. First, activities of real managers are much more diverse. In addition, implementing all five functions often takes more clout than most RMs have.

Fayol then clothed his five functions in the following fourteen principles of management that worked (for him):

1. Division of Work. Specialization makes functional division of the organization and functionally oriented education and training possible. In fact, work is never perfectly divided either by required effort or skills. When real managers control resources essential to do work, they have more power than others who control fewer, or less important, resources. Hence, the division of work is affected by both functional (need to get the job done) considerations, as described by Fayol, and political (power and control) considerations. Real managers address the latter through their networking activities.

2. Equal Authority and Responsibility. If managers have responsibility for a given area, they should have the commensurate authority to carry it out. In fact, real managers are usually restricted on both counts. They often have limited control over the consequences if subordinates do not perform. Most RMs today do not control the hiring, firing, pay, or promotion of their subordinates directly. This again means real managers must cope with the problem by maximizing their own reservoir of human resource management and networking skills.

3. Discipline. Obedience and outward respect are two tenets of traditional management that still seem to be relevant to many of the organizations we studied.

4. Unity of Command. The one-boss principle is really a myth in some of the organizations we studied.

5. Unity of Direction. Groups or individuals with the same purposes and objectives are ideal but rarely found in the organizations we studied.

6. Subordination of Personal Interest to General Interest. For the short run, this principle of traditional management may hold, but for the long run it denies the realities of human behavior. Even apparently "selfless" real managers operate from a base of educated self-interest. They seem to exchange short-term for long-term returns. In contemporary society, long-run subordination of an RM's self-interest may be unrealistic: it would require that RMs be irrationally oblivious to their own interests.

7. Remuneration of Personnel. The amount of remuneration still is determined largely by the value of the manager to the organization, as adjusted for labor market conditions.

8. Centralization. Directly related to "Equal Authority and Responsibility," this principle states that when the mid-level RM's job becomes important enough, upper level management (eventually) relinquishes sufficient power for the RM to get the job done.

9. Scalar Chain. The chain exists, but real managers supplement it by crossing department and division boundaries in day-to-day activities. Without the networking relationships and "dotted lines," probably nothing in these organizations would get done.

10. Order. With a degree of order, RMs and equipment, for example, have specific office, telephone, and storage locations where we can expect to find them. However, because of the dynamic nature of many of the organizations studied, chaos, not order, reigned supreme.

11. Equity. Employees demand fairness (on balance, not necessarily on every issue), as *they* see it. Except for the cases of assimilating women and minorities into the mainstream of organizational life, RMs respond to, if not take affirmative action for, this critical need in day-to-day activities.

12. Stability of Tenure of Personnel. Real managers should seek to develop cadres of subordinates committed to long-term employment. Japanese firms with their life-time employment policies illustrate this principle; there is evidence that many American firms do also. However, rapidly changing technology, resistance to change (by the organization as well as by individual employees), and overhead costs of employee medical and retirement benefits seem to drive many real managers to pursue short-run or intermediate (rather than long-term) work force objectives.

13. Initiative. RMs should be encouraged to be self-activating. Tom Peters, of *In Search of Excellence* fame, feels strongly that constant innovation is a basic requirement for successful, effective management. We found that most RMs find themselves in dynamically changing situations today; they should be aware of this inherent potential for initiative and innovation.

14. Esprit de corps. Harmony and commitment among employees are the objectives of this principle. Some of the organizations we studied had flirted with organization development (OD), and more recently quality of work life (QWL) programs. The RMs generally reacted positively to these programs but felt they didn't last long enough to make an impact. Other things, such as budgets and cutbacks, took precedence.

Besides Fayol, other classical management theorists and all the introductory management textbooks in the field today list similar principles to follow for success and effectiveness. In fact, there are probably as many ideas about what managers should do as there are managers— maybe more! Prescriptions and advice have been offered not only by management scholars and writers but also by psychologists, sociologists, economists, political scientists, business scholars in finance and marketing, and sometimes even practicing managers themselves.

THE MANAGEMENT JUNGLE

The late Harold Koontz described the widely divergent principles and theories of management as a "jungle." Koontz's famous article, "The Management Theory Jungle," was one "map" to follow out of the jungle. He described six schools of management, which we will describe as "waterholes in the jungle."

Waterhole No. 1: The Management Process School. This approach begins by identifying functions of managers (a la Fayol's plan, organize, command, coordinate, and control). It then asks questions about the nature, purpose, structure, and processes of each function and formulates universal principles (a la Fayol's fourteen principles). As we discussed above, this is often unrealistic material for real managers.

Waterhole No. 2: The Empirical School. This is an experiential approach, based on cases and observations of what worked in the past and might be reapplied when needed in the future. This approach was used by management scholars to regenerate "universal" principles of management by following the same steps as the management process approach. If we duplicate this case approach, the return on investment for RMs is not very great.

Waterhole No. 3: The Human Behavior School. This approach centers on interpersonal relations, in the guises of human relations, leadership, or organizational psychology. We found this to be a good approach for some of the problems facing today's real managers. This approach is becoming more important as technology has outstripped management of human resources recently.

Waterhole No. 4: The Social System School. This approach focuses on social and cultural issues, not necessarily restricting them to those of the formal organization. Essentially, the approach seeks to apply to management the principles of basic sociology, social, and group behavior and, more recently, cultural anthropology. Unfortunately, real managers have not yet been able to translate much of such behavioral science knowledge into action, therefore, it doesn't offer real protection from day-to-day threats facing RMs in the jungle.

Waterhole No. 5: The Decision Theory School. This school emphasizes quantifying (assigning numbers to) management problems or courses of action and rationally selecting the best, or optimal, solution. Based on an economics foundation, it springs from problems in utility maximization, indifference curves, marginal utility, and risk/uncertainty behavior. This approach offers protection to RMs from some, but certainly not all, threats in the management jungle.

Waterhole No. 6: The Mathematical School. This approach focuses on using mathematical logic to express and solve problems in management mathematically. Unfortunately, RMs aren't able to reduce their problems to such logical statements. Perhaps much of what happens in the day-to-day activities of real managers, if for no other reason than lack of information, is "illogical." Again, mathematics can help save RMs from some, but not all, jungle perils.

Can we escape from the jungle of confusion? Taking the extremes seems unwise. If we view each management approach, or school, as correct unto itself, then we will discard whatever may be useful in each of the rejected approaches. The other extreme view, that we must take a global view of *everything* offered by *all* of the approaches and that none of it will be of value unless and until we make it all work together, also seems fruitless. Each of these extremes points the way back into the jungle.

The correct path is to use the benefits of each approach, tempered by what real managers actually do, and first to determine what successful and effective RMs do before we endorse prescriptive approaches of what managers *should* do.

The next two chapters will analyze the activities identified in this chapter for empirically defined successful RMs (Chapter 3) and effective RMs (Chapter 4). The subsequent chapters will then give specific attention, in turn, to the traditional management activities (Chapter 5), communication activities (Chapter 6), networking activities (Chapter 7), and human resource management activities (Chapter 8).

3 WHAT DO SUCCESSFUL REAL MANAGERS DO?

Just as there has been considerable literature on what managers supposedly do, there has also been much written over the years about the essential ingredients for managerial success. Nearly every management book presumes that effective performance is the goal and that a manager's success goes hand-in-hand with being effective. Often the terms "successful" and "effective" are used interchangeably; however, as we pointed out in Chapter 1, we do not treat these terms as synonyms. Although there are some important exceptions and fine points, we have found major differences between what effective real managers do (the focus of the next chapter), and what successful real managers do (the focus of this chapter).

Lee Iacocca says of being the best or the most successful, "What else is there?" We have found common threads, common activities that RMs do in order to become "the best." The question then becomes one of "the best" for whom—the manager or the organization that employs the manager? And what does "the best" really mean—successful or effective RMs? After first reviewing the few attempts that have been made to analyze managerial success, we will present our analysis and findings. Then, as in Chapter 2, we will explode some of the prevailing myths surrounding how one gets ahead in organizations.

THE LACK OF PREVIOUS WORK ON MANAGERIAL SUCCESS

There are many biographies and autobiographies of prominent managers and leaders. These include elected government officials and cabinet members, as well as CEOs in the private sector such as Lee Iacocca (Chrysler), Henry Ford II (Ford Motor), and Harold Geneen (ITT). However, there has been very little systematic study about what real managers do. As Chapter 2 detailed, Mintzberg and others have studied what managers really do, but they did not isolate what *successful* managers do. In addition, the little research that has been done on the nature of managerial work has often depended on survey questionnaires. When direct observation has been done, as in the cases of the work of Mintzberg and Kotter, the sample sizes have been very small. Such studies do not allow comparison of the relative success of the managers studied.

BACKGROUND ON THE MANAGERIAL SUCCESS ANALYSIS

In traditional management literature as well as to the person on the street, the meaning of "success" is an individual one. Therefore, the question, "What do successful managers really do?" must be posed as an empirical research question. Unlike our preliminary work with hundreds of RMs from many different types of organizations, the success portion of the study required more control, so we drew from a sample of fifty-two RMs from a limited number of organizations. This sample was used to determine if the type of organization or the level of the manager made a difference in relative success. However, we did analyze an additional sample of seventy-nine RMs drawn from a wide range of organizations and found similar results regarding the impact of managerial activities related to success to the sample of fifty-two RMs. It should be emphasized that these samples were drawn from the 248 RMs whose behavior was recorded by the trained participant observers. Thus, the observers were blind to whether the target RMs were defined as successful or not.

Before starting the study of successful RMs, we reasoned that a consensus about what success "is," would always be what the scholar or the practitioner thinks that success "should" be. We further reasoned that each organization has its own measure of managerial success, that the most "successful" managers are those most valued by their organizations, and that each organization rewards its most "successful" managers. The most substantive and direct way that organizations do this is through promotion. Therefore, the measure of managerial success that we used is an indicator of what the employing organization has already declared to be a "success." It is based on a promotion index or the speed (or velocity) of promotion.

THE MEASURE OF SUCCESS USED

We developed a "manager success index" (MSI) for the real managers in our analysis of successful managers. This measure was derived from previous approaches used to determine either promotion velocity or manager achievement. In our study, we calculated the MSI for each RM in our sample based on the level of the RM in the organization divided by the RM's tenure in the organization. (The interested reader may want to refer to the 1986 Luthans, Rosenkrantz, and Hennessey article cited in the supplemental readings and references for a more detailed description of the MSI.)

One of the first arguments against such a measure as the MSI is that it does not account for new hires at high levels, who clearly have a short tenure with the organization. However, it should be noted that the organization assesses the value of new hires before employing them. By the organization's own definition, the new hire, under such conditions, has greater perceived value and consequent rewards (that is, success) than longer tenured in-house managers; otherwise, the longer tenured managers would have been promoted faster (and promotion would have occurred from within the organization). Therefore, high MSIs for newly hired managers are not unlikely. The MSI is also useful because middle- or even lower level managers also could be "successful" by this index, depending on how long they had been with the organization.

We have cross-checked the effects on our findings using MSI, relative pay, and level, but disregarding tenure in the organization, and have found comparable results. However, note that successful managers, as defined by the MSI, may be at the top, middle or lower levels of their organizations. In other words, an RM who is at the third level from the top but has been with the company for only six years is deemed to be more successful than another RM at the second level who has been with the company for twenty years. In addition, in some of our analyses of successful managers, we simply defined the CEO, the head of the organization, as being successful. (By definition, or using our index [first level], the CEO is successful.)

ACTIVITIES OF SUCCESSFUL REAL MANAGERS

Our analysis of successful real managers took several directions. In the first part of our investigation we identified the specific managerial activities that statistically were related to success (using multiple regression techniques) as defined by the MSI. Further analysis was done to see if the type of organization or the level of the RM made a difference. Next, we did a descriptive comparison of the activities of the most successful third of the RMs in the organizations studied with the activities of the least successful third. Because we wanted to analyze only those who were clearly successful or unsuccessful, the middle third was left out of the comparison analysis. We also compared what activities top-level RMs do with what activities mid-level and first-level RMs do. Finally, we determined the relative strength of the managerial activities related to RMs' success.

Importance of Networking Activities

One of the most revealing and definitive findings of the entire study was the importance of networking to managerial success. As identified in Chapter 2, the networking activity consisted of "interacting with outsiders" and "socializing and politicking." Behaviorally, "interacting with outsiders" was defined in the study as interacting with customers, suppliers and outside contacts; attending external meetings; and doing public relations and community service activities. For example, one successful RM told us he had a deliberate two-prong strategy of calling on his supplier rather than always having the supplier call on him, and spending at least one afternoon a week visiting his customers, unannounced, to see what problems they were having with his firm's service. This same manager was on the board of the local YMCA and regularly attended the Rotary Club.

"Socializing and politicking" was behaviorally defined in the study as nonwork-related "chit chat" concerning family or personal matters; informal joking; discussing rumors, hearsay, and the grapevine; complaining, griping, and downgrading others; and doing politicking and gamesmanship. Besides the formal analysis, we picked up from interviews and informal interactions with successful RMs and their subordinates how skillful they were at socializing, politicking, and interacting with outsiders and how much time they spent in this activity. One real manager elaborated:

> People in this place get tired of always talking about business. They would rather talk about football or the latest rumor. I find that if I deliberately talk about these things either with my subordinates or the guy in the finance department, I can get in better with them and then call on them when I need them to meet a deadline or vote my way in a committee meeting.

Thus, this successful RM does socializing and politicking in order to develop contacts, relationships, and reciprocal networks that magnify his available resources and ability to deliver when needed.

Further Analysis by Organization and Level

Importantly, statistical analysis clearly revealed that networking, more than any of the other activities, was most closely related to managerial success. The "interacting with outsiders" dimension of networking was found to be related to success in all the organizations studied in the success analysis. "Socializing and politicking," on the other hand, was found to be related to success more closely in entrepreneurial and results-oriented organizations than in bureaucratic and highly formalized organizations. This is not surprising. For example, when an important decision is to be made and there is uncertainty surrounding it (as in an unstructured situation with little or no experience of formal policies or rules), there are more attempts to influence the outcome through political maneuvering. When the decision is certain (as in a highly structured situation with considerable experience and formal policies or rules to cover it), there are fewer attempts to influence the outcome through socializing and politicking.

Our findings suggest that successful RMs do not dissipate their time and energies dealing with what they know to be uncontrollable variables. Therefore, they would be expected to adapt their networking strategies to fit different types of organizations. Top-level managers tend to support this conclusion with how frequently (or how infrequently) they exhibit these activities. For example, top-level, CEO RMs interact with outsiders about as often as middle-level RMs but nearly three times as often as first-level RMs. But the frequency is reversed for socializing and politicking. Middle-level and first-level RMs socialize and politick nearly three times as often as do the top-level RMs in our study. The logic behind this is simply that socializing and politicking may have been necessary to get to the top, but once there it is no longer a necessary activity.

MOST VERSUS LEAST SUCCESSFUL
REAL MANAGERS

Besides doing statistical analysis to determine which activities were significantly related to managerial success, we next did a simple descriptive comparative analysis between the most successful (top third on the promotion index) and the least successful (bottom third on the promotion index).

It should be noted at the outset that *all* the RMs at all levels did considerable amounts of all of the managerial activities that we measured. That is, they all did the traditional management activities of planning, decisionmaking, and controlling; communication activities of processing paperwork and exchanging routine information; networking activities of interacting with outsiders and socializing/politicking; and human resource management activities of managing conflict, staffing, training/developing, motivating/reinforcing, and disciplining/punishing. Although we found significant differences in the amounts of these activities for the more versus less successful RMs, the differences do not imply that successful managers engaged in activities that less successful managers did not do at all (or vice versa).

This analysis does not necessarily mean that the activities we measured by directly observing the RMs are the sine qua non factors for more or less managerial success. The findings could also mean that the directly observable activities we identified are merely representative of other, related characteristics that were not part of our study. For example, RMs who devote their energies to developing a power base through networking may be doing so because of their raw intelligence and/or perseverance (characteristics commonly held to be related to managerial success). But, as we have said before, our study differs from previous research in that we used the frequency counts of directly observable activities of real managers in their day-to-day activities. A breakdown of these activities comparing the most versus the least successful RMs is summarized in Figure 3–1.

Figure 3-1. More versus Less Successful Managers (Drawn from top third and bottom third of 52 RMs).

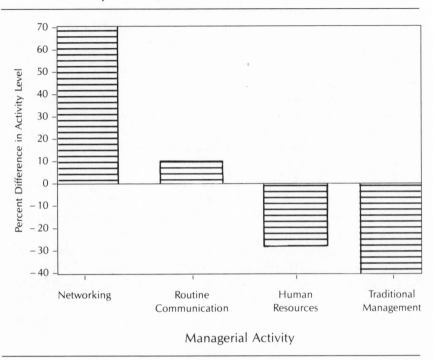

The bars in Figure 3-1 represent the percent of difference in frequencies of the managerial activities of the most successful (top third using the promotion index) compared to least successful RMs (the bottom third using the promotion index.) Thus, Figure 3-1 indicates that the "most successful" RMs are doing 70 percent more networking activities and 10 percent more routine communication activities than the "least successful" RMs. However, the most successful RMs are doing 25 percent less human resources activities and 40 percent less traditional management activities than the least successful RMs.

RELATIVE STRENGTHS OF THE MANAGERIAL ACTIVITIES' RELATIONSHIP TO RM SUCCESS

In addition to doing the statistical and comparative analysis, we determined the relative strengths of the managerial activities' relationship to RM success. We calculated the correlations squared between each of the eleven observed activities and the success index (MSI) and then rank ordered these relationships in terms of their relative strengths. The components of the four major activities were then averaged. The result for the same sample (N = 52 managers) that was used in both the statistical analysis and comparative analysis is shown in Figure 3–2. This shows the relative strengths of the relationship between the managerial activities and RM success. The contribution of these relationships to RM success is an indication of their relative pay-off toward success. In other words, some activities seem to contribute more to success than others.

As shown, networking activities once again had the strongest relationship to the success of RMs. Networking was followed, in turn, by communication, traditional management, and human resource management activities. A more detailed breakdown revealed that socializing/politicking had by far the strongest relationship and interacting with outsiders was third. The communication activity of exchanging routine information was second.

Note that only descriptive relationships are indicated, and that causal conclusions, such as that networking leads to success, are not warranted in this analysis. Also keep in mind that a sample of fifty-two RMs, and not all the RMs from the four-year study, were used in this "success" part of the study. However, in this part of the analysis, we did add in another

Figure 3–2. Relative Contributions to Manager Success (N = 52 RMs, using data on relative strength of relationship between managerial activities and RM success).

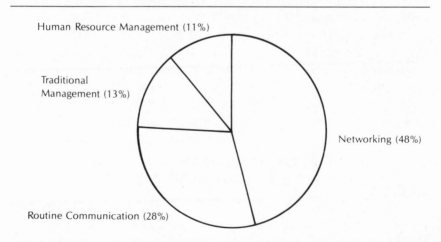

sample of seventy-nine RMs from a number of diverse organizations and obtained almost identical results to those shown in Figure 3–2.

Of particular interest is the fact that all three analytic techniques—statistical, comparative, and relative strength of relationship—revealed the same finding: the importance of the networking activity to successful RMs. In addition, all analyses showed that successful RMs also do relatively more routine communication activities.

Surprisingly, human resource management activities and traditional management activities were observed less frequently in the successful RMs than in the unsuccessful RMs in the comparative analysis, and similarly came out last in the strength of relationship analysis. This finding refutes those who have advocated a human resource management approach and the importance of doing the traditional management functions. Could it be that successful RMs give less attention to human resources and traditional management than do their unsuccessful counterparts? This important finding embodies the purpose of this book—discovering empirically, perhaps for the first time, what real managers are all about. We will explore the ramifications of these findings more thoroughly but first will discuss each of the activities in relation to successful RMs.

Networking Activities of Successful RMs

Subordinates of successful RMs described their boss's networking activities in the following ways:

> Jim is constantly seeking and nurturing contacts inside and outside the firm. He is always friendly and seems interested in your personal life. I like him and would do anything for him.

> We get along real well in this department because we know George has such clout upstairs, as well as in the community, that no one is going to bother us.

As indicated, all levels of analysis substantiated the prime importance that networking activities (socializing/politicking and interacting with outsiders) hold for successful RMs. This finding held regardless of the type of organization or the RM's level in the organization. Successful RMs do more networking than their less successful counterparts. Figure 3–1 showed that successful RMs engage in this activity 70 percent more than their unsuccessful counterparts. The relationship analysis shown in Figure 3–2 indicated that networking is almost as strong as the other three activities combined. Chapter 7 is devoted to this important, but traditionally overlooked, managerial activity.

Routine Communication Activities of Successful RMs

As indicated in the comparative analysis in Figure 3–1, successful RMs do slightly more (about 10 percent) routine communication activities (exchanging routine information and paperwork) than their unsuccessful counterparts. Also, in the relationship analysis, Figure 3–2 showed that communication is clearly the second strongest ingredient in RM success. These findings do support the assumed importance of communication skills to managerial success and complement the networking activities of successful RMs.

When the two major behavioral categories in this routine communication activity were examined closely, it was found that exchanging routine information accounted for most of the difference between successful and unsuccessful RMs in the comparative analysis. The attention given to paperwork between the two groups was about the same, as shown in both the comparative analysis and the relationship analysis. After the networking activity of socializing/politicking, exchanging routine information had the strongest relationship with successful RMs. The other communication activity of handling paperwork fell in the middle in terms of relative strength of the relationship.

These findings make sense. Successful RMs are asking for and giving information more often than their unsuccessful counterparts. Successful RMs do the required paperwork, meet deadlines for reports, and cover themselves in a political sense, but they do not seem to put a priority on paperwork. One manager elaborated:

> I like to keep informed and I like to keep my people informed. Mostly I do this verbally rather than in writing. I prefer to pick up the phone or drop by my people's desks to tell them something or ask them something. I don't write them memos. Unfortunately, that doesn't mean that there is no paperwork in this job. I try to keep up with my in-box and meet all deadlines for reports and requests from the boss. If I don't do at least that much, I look bad, as if I'm letting things slip.

When analyzed by type of organization and level of the RM in the organizations, there were no appreciable differences in the communication activities. Thus, like networking, successful RMs in the organizations in the sample, and at all levels of these organizations, did more communication activities. Chapter 6 discusses the communication activities in more detail.

Human Resources Management Activities of Successful RMs

The behaviorally oriented management literature stresses the unqualified importance of human resources management activities. However, one of the most striking findings of our study is that successful managers do not seem to be doing nearly as much of these activities as the less successful managers. This result was indicated in both the comparative analysis and the relative strength of relationship analysis. Successful managers are doing more networking and communication and less human resource management activities. These findings present an interesting and revealing profile of managerial success.

The management literature in general, and research in organizational behavior and human resources management in particular, maintains that human resource management activities are necessary for *effective* management. Yet our findings showed that *successful* RMs are doing less of these activities than their unsuccessful counterparts. Obviously, there are tremendous implications if *effective* RMs do human resource management activities but *successful* RMs do not. Chapter 4 will present how human resource management activities fit into the profile of effective RMs and will explore the implications of the difference between success and effectiveness.

There are several possible explanations why successful RMs give less attention to human resource activities. For example, perhaps successful RMs are more task- or achievement-oriented, an outlook that is incompatible with a human approach. It is also possible that a "lag effect," as proposed by organizational psychologist Rensis Likert, is at work.

The rationale behind Likert's "lag effect" is that the work unit is managed, over time, by successions of managers, some of whom take a human resources approach and some who don't. He believes, and his survey evidence supports, that the manager who uses human resource management activities will be more effective, but it takes time (that is, there is a "lag") for this to work itself out. Top management (those making promotions) often are impatient and do not let a human-oriented manager stay long enough for the lag to take effect. Top management then brings in an autocratic (what Likert called a Systems I) manager to tighten the ship. This coincides with the effectiveness generated by the previous human resources manager finally taking hold. Thus, the autocratic manager inherits an effective work unit, resulting in a promotion. It is also possible for the incoming autocratic manager to exploit the work unit for his or her short-term gain, exiting with a promotion and leaving an ineffective work unit. His human-oriented successor then inherits the ineffective work unit, which takes considerable time to reclaim, reflecting badly on the new manager and impeding his or her chances for promotion, regardless of how much attention is given to the human resources activities. Once subordinate trust is violated, it can take even a human-oriented successor considerable time to repair the damage and restore desired levels of work unit effectiveness.

A Closer Look at the Human Resource Management Activities

Breaking the human resource activity into its component behavioral categories for closer examination was much more revealing than it was for networking and communicating. Of particular interest was managing conflict (behaviorally defined in the study as managing interpersonal conflicts, appealing to higher authority to resolve a dispute, appealing to third-party negotiators, trying to get cooperation or consensus, attempting to resolve conflicts between a subordinate and oneself). This human resource management activity was very strongly associated with successful RMs in the comparative analysis and had a moderately strong relationship in the relative strength analysis. Subordinates described successful RMs managing conflict activities in the following way:

> He often tries to prevent conflict by watching for red flags and then quickly bringing the parties together to come up with a solution before a big fight erupts.

> My manager knows how to smooth out conflicts between us. She will listen to both sides and then try to solve the problem so we both think we won.

Further analysis, however, revealed that the managing conflict resource activity varied considerably with the type of organization and the level of the RM. For example, one of the organizations we studied in depth was a heterogeneous manufacturing plant that was differentiated by departments, jobs, people, and "profit centers." There was considerable ambiguity about "turf," authority, and responsibilities, especially in the middle- and lower level manager ranks. In this organization the successful RMs exhibited considerably more behaviors identified as managing conflict than did their unsuccessful counterparts. One manager explained:

> We are always competing for resources in this department. I have to spend a lot of my time trying to smooth things out and make sure *all* the projects meet the deadlines and quality specs. The only way I know how to do this is to act as a mediator and keep things fair for all concerned. Everyone is under pressure and my job is to help interpret the gray areas and keep everybody together for our overall company goals.

Two other organizations we studied in this part of the analysis were public sector organizations: a state department of revenue and a campus police department. In contrast to the manufacturing plant, these public sector organizations were highly formalized and mechanistic. There were many more bureaucratic rules and legal statutes, leaving less in doubt, less "up for grabs," and less likelihood of crossing territorial boundaries (treading on someone else's turf) to get the job done. In both of these organizations, the successful RMs exhibited considerably less of this managing conflict human resource activity than did their unsuccessful counterparts. Thus, this analysis by type of organization indicates that when the organizational structure clearly defines job roles, particularly in a stable environment, the ability or effort a manager devotes to managing conflict may not lead to success; however, in ill-defined, ambiguous situations, managing conflict may lend itself to success.

In addition to the type of organization, the level of the RM also has an impact on whether managing conflict is associated with success. In particular, further analysis indicated that top-level RMs manage conflict much more often than do either mid- or first-level RMs. It may be that top-level RMs are more attentive, or at least sensitive, to dysfunctional conflict and thus give more effort to it. They are more disposed to be peacemakers. It could also mean that top-level positions tend to be closer to significant territorial disputes because middle- and lower level RMs, who may work without well-defined rules and boundaries, especially in certain types of organizations, feel this is just part of the job and make no special effort to manage conflict.

When we analyzed the other human resource management activities more closely, we found in the comparative analysis that training/developing was done equally by successful and unsuccessful managers.

However, motivating/reinforcing was done a surprising 30 percent less by successful RMs and staffing was done a whopping 70 percent less by the successful RMs. In the relative strength of relationship analysis, motivating/reinforcing had a moderately strong relationship, but, echoing the comparative analysis, both staffing and training/developing had a very weak relationship with success. Unlike managing conflict, neither the type of organization nor the level of the RM affected these results. The relative lack of human resource management activities done by the successful RMs is one of the most important findings in our study; its implications for organizational effectiveness and subordinate productivity will serve as a point of departure in the analysis and conclusions of subsequent chapters.

Again, keep in mind that the analyses do not indicate causal relationships. For example, the very weak showing of the staffing activity could possibly be attributed to successful RMs being so well organized that they do not have to reconfigure or reschedule very often. For example, turnover and absenteeism may be low, their subordinates may get to work on time, and successful RMs may not need to find replacements very often. If someone should quit or be absent, there may be contingency plans to handle the load or predetermined work priorities that permit some work to be deferred until the vacancy is filled. Less successful managers may lack the freedom or the ability to make such plans or priorities.

Planning for short-run personnel shortages, such as allowing for absentees, justifiable lateness, or vacations, reduces ambiguity and job stress. For example, when vacations are not realistically planned into the schedule, employees in many work units are expected to complete the work left undone during their vacations. RMs with this kind of perspective about staffing may also create high rates of turnover, absenteeism, and tardiness. Conversely, realistic staffing may contribute to satisfied subordinates, reduced turnover, absenteeism and tardiness. When all of these positive trends are developing, some semblance of fairness prevails that may reduce the staffing requirements for successful RMs.

The more obvious explanation, of course, is simply that successful managers do relatively less of these human resource management activities. The implications of this finding for organizational effectiveness and subordinate satisfaction will be detailed in the subsequent chapters.

Traditional Management Activities of Successful RMs

As Figure 3-1 showed, the traditional management activities fared even worse than the human resource management activities in the comparative analysis. Successful RMs did 40 percent less of these activities than did their unsuccessful counterparts. Also, on the relative strength of relationship analysis, Figure 3-2 showed that the traditional management activities were tied with the human resources management activities for the weakest relationships with managerial success. Three behavioral categories constitute these traditional management activities: decisionmaking, planning, and controlling.

Decisionmaking. The traditional management activity of decisionmaking may be overemphasized. We found it to be much narrower in scope and importance for our successful RMs than much of the management literature decrees. Real managers do not make glamorous economic decisions or those that determine the fate of multinational conglomerates, as so often portrayed in textbooks and business classes. Nor do they decide whether their organization will attempt a stock takeover of another corporation, how to defend themselves against a hostile stock takeover, or overall corporate strategy and policy. Instead, as Chapter 2 pointed out, real managers make many modest or even insignificant decisions that are nevertheless essential to daily, weekly, and monthly operations of their areas of responsibility.

Even though the decisionmaking activity is presumed important, our comparative analysis found that the most successful third of the RMs devoted about the same effort to making decisions as did the least successful third. The relative strength of relationship analysis found decision making even less dominant than the comparative analysis. Only planning and the human resource management activities had weaker relationships to success. Although the type of organization does not seem to matter, as in the managing conflict activity, further analysis revealed that the relation of decisionmaking to successful managers did seem to depend on the level of the RM.

As one would suspect, decisionmaking opportunities and authority graduate by level, increasing as the manager moves upward in the organizational hierarchy. At least on this activity, a traditional management perspective may be at work. At lower levels, formalization and structure (through rules and regulations) may reduce the manager's decision-making opportunities drastically. Further analysis revealed that top-level RMs do much more decisionmaking than do mid- or first-level RMs. This indicates that bureaucratic hierarchy and chain-of-command authority limit the amount of decisionmaking possible. Top-level RMs have more decisionmaking *opportunities* than have RMs at lower levels; as a "step function," the difference in decisionmaking opportunities changes sharply, rather than gradually, in each step of the hierarchy.

At top-level management, where the work is less routine, decisions must be made more often. Lower level decisionmaking is reduced through bureaucratic policies, rules, and regulations or may even be taken over by computerization. One manager commented:

> Sure, I would like to be able to make more decisions and solve problems to show my boss that I am executive material. But in this job I have very little discretion. I have to go by what the numbers say or by existing policy handed down to me. I seldom have a chance to make a decision.

Chapter 5 will give more detailed attention to decisionmaking and other dimensions of the traditional management activities of RMs.

Planning.   A closer look at the comparative analysis reveals that the more successful RMs were observed to do less planning than their unsuccessful counterparts. In the relative strength of relationship investigation, planning had the weakest relationship with success of all the activities studied. Once again, type of organization seems to make little difference but, as in the decisionmaking finding, when success was defined as the top-level manager, it was found that top-level RMs do much more planning than mid-level RMs or first-level RMs. This further analysis, therefore, does support traditional notions about the importance of planning for at least top-level executives. Nevertheless, the overall findings have several interesting insights into the question of what do successful RMs do.

First, the traditional management literature fails to mention whether some functions, planning for example, are more or less important at different levels of management. Although the recent strategic planning literature definitely focuses on top management, the traditional theories were given as universal truths applicable to all levels. We discovered that this may be an oversimplification. A second implication of our results is to recognize that because of external forces, such as the economy or technological complexity or change, many organizations now centralize the planning function. This leaves less opportunity for planning at lower levels.

Third, less successful managers may be doing more planning than more successful managers, but at the expense of other important activities. For example, networking or communicating activities may affect managerial success more directly than planning activities. A subordinate described an unsuccessful manager's planning activity this way:

> He always has us busy inputting into the long-range plan for the department. He seems to be spinning his wheels in this regard. However, his counterpart over in the sales department seems conveniently to ignore the long-range plan and is busy politicking with the boss for more resources and keeping his people informed on a daily basis.

Fourth, planning seems to be a skill that is not equally well developed among all managers. Such qualitative differences among managers as planners mean that the frequency (amount) of doing planning activity does not distinguish the successful (best) from the less successful (mediocre) manager. The quality of a plan lies in whether it can feasibly and efficiently be translated into bottom-line results. Less successful managers may be spending more time preparing ineffective plans, planning the wrong things, or substituting plans for real performance.

Finally, the less successful RMs may be spending more time planning in order to overprotect themselves (for example, to evade responsibility for things that happen, or because of lack of confidence in subordinates). Chapter 5 will give further attention to the planning activities of RMs.

Controlling.   The traditional management activity of controlling fared even worse than decisionmaking and planning in the comparative success analysis but better in the relative strength of relationship analysis. The top third of successful RMs were observed to do controlling much less than the bottom third of unsuccessful RMs, but the relative strength of the relationship of this activity to success put it in the middle of all the managerial activities. Again, the type of organization does not seem to matter, but when success was defined as the top-level manager, we found that top-level managers control less than those at the middle level and first level.

The traditional perspective, of course, is that performing the control function is an activity that is primary to a manager's success. We would certainly not argue against the contribution the control activity can make to managerial success, but our results suggest that the efficiency of the method of control may be more important than how much a manager is directly involved in the process of control. In particular, the following implications seem to follow from our results on the control activity:

1. An optimum level of controlling performance may be recognized by more successful RMs and even more by top-level RMs. They may be able to adjust the amount of personal control that is required by altering the control systems and the work environments. This is done by influencing their superiors, maintaining effective relationships with subordinates, developing consistency (even routinizing change), delegating, and distributing written policies and procedures. These activities complement the networking and communicating activities and help RMs stabilize their work environments. These approaches may accomplish more controlling with less direct effort, thereby freeing managers for other important activities.

2. The control activity is a high-risk function. Because success depends on other people, as evidenced by the importance of networking, the RM whose performance is more dependent on controlling the performance of others may be at greater risk of failure than the RM whose performance is less dependent on others. Control can be a negative experience; a real manager who must devote a lot of time and effort to it, because of the nature of the job or because of style, may not win many friends or influence the powerful others necessary to success.

RM SUCCESS RESULTS IN PERSPECTIVE

Chapter 2 uncovered some interesting answers to the question of what do real managers do. Chapter 3 found some equally interesting, and perhaps more startling, answers to the question of what do successful real managers do. In particular, successful RMs do networking and, to a lesser degree, communicating activities. Contrary to management literature, successful managers do not seem to be doing as much human resource management and traditional management activities as their unsuccessful counterparts. In light of these results, let's reexamine some of the myths surrounding managerial success.

EXPLODING THE MYTHS OF MANAGERIAL SUCCESS

The standard analysis of managerial success has always assumed that certain personal traits and/or managerial activities "cause" managers to succeed. Just as Chapter 2 debunked some of the myths of what managers do, we have found that what successful RMs actually do also differs from what traditional management literature says they "should" do in order to be successful.

What is Traditionally Meant by Success?

There are probably as many ideas and prescriptions about what a manager should do to be successful as there are writings on the subject. These range all the way from a Dale Carnegie course brochure to a research-based article or book on organizational behavior. The definition of managerial success becomes crucial. Although it is easy to detect the fluff of simplistic "how-to" approaches to success, the research-based "scholarly" writings can be just as misleading and irrelevant to real managers.

In some organizations under some conditions, task-oriented managers prosper and are successful; in other organizations, and even in the same organization under different conditions, a manager using such a style cannot even survive. The same finding holds for people-oriented managers. The so-called contingency approach to management tries to account for these situational differences, but does it mean, as one RM put it, that "the way managers succeed makes no sense?" Or could it mean that a given style or behavior or activity affects success only indirectly?

Willy Loman, the lead character in *Death of a Salesman,* defined success as whether or not the manager ". . . was well liked." We may question the merit of such a simplistic definition of manager success, but when researchers ask subordinates in a questionnaire survey subjectively to report on their managers, they are really using the same approach suggested by Willy's definition of success.

In defining what makes a successful manager, we must ask who is doing the defining. In the conventional textbook and research arena, academicians typically depend on prior evidence and their own best judgment to decide what personal characteristics and managerial activities best describe a successful manager. Similarly, practicing managers use their experience and best judgment to determine those characteristics and activities. In reality, practicing managers don't have the time, or don't take the time, to define what makes a manager successful because they are too busy getting the job done. They, rightly or wrongly, believe that events eventually will determine managerial success at the bottom line.

The problem with both academic and practitioner approaches to managerial success is that they are based on assumptions, or at best, quasi-empirical evidence from survey research, experience, or even intuition. Let's reexamine some of these common assumptions about managerial success in light of findings on successful RMs.

The Myth of Shared Psychological Characteristics

One school of thought in the management literature suggests that successful managers share common psychological characteristics such as the following:

1. a strong need to achieve (or n-ach);
2. a strong need to obtain and use power (or n-pow);
3. a relatively weak need for affiliation (or n-aff);
4. complex reasoning patterns, the ability to process a great deal of information; and
5. relatively high intelligence.

Although some successful managers undoubtedly have these characteristics, there has been no evidence to date to suggest that *successful* managers possess them in greater (or lesser) amounts than unsuccessful managers. (Harvard psychologist David McClelland has conducted research relating n-ach and n-pow to *effective* managers.) Presumably, all good managers have a strong need to achieve. However, this motivation can be situationally specific with regard to the success of the high n-ach manager. For example, in many highly structured public service jobs, it is possible for managers to rise to high-level positions without a strong need to achieve (for example, by a political payoff). It is even conceivable that by demonstrating unusual achievement motivation, such managers might be regarded as a threat to their contemporaries, superiors, or "the system," resulting in career failure, rather than career success.

One of our real managers fit this description. His ambition was to retire on a small farm on the southern Pacific coast and to supplement his retirement income with income from the farm. He was an upper-level manager whose primary job was to ensure that essential new equipment was located and acquired for a very large Federal agency operating in a fairly unstable environment. His purview included budgets of hundreds of millions of dollars. Before assuming this responsible job, he had performed routine duties for his entire twenty-seven-year career in the civil service. He was elevated to his current position, in his own assessment as well as that of others who knew him, seemingly on the strength of his benign personality (he was "well liked"). This position had historically been a final stepping-stone to top-level management and was usually reserved for entrepreneurial managers with extraordinarily strong needs to achieve and to distinguish themselves. However, this RM did not fit the mold: he operated in a "caretaker" role until he quietly retired three years later.

Here is a case in which top-level management had decided that they could afford to sacrifice a position as "soft-core" (marginally productive) in order to provide a holding area for a mediocre senior manager until he retired. In fact, this RM was selected because he was not a threat to the manager one level above (who had himself been assigned as a consequence of failure in his previous job). The point is not that there is no "justice" or "logic" to managerial success, nor that what makes a manager successful is beyond understanding, but that we may be thinking of success in inappropriate, or too logical, ways.

It is easy to dismiss the analysis of success in this example as being typical of government jobs but not of business and industry standards of success. Yet doesn't the same thing occur in organizations in the private sector, where there is often no clear accountability for performance? We found many successful RMs who seemed to defy traditional ideas about what psychological traits are needed for managerial success.

The Myth That Subordinate Satisfaction Relates to Managerial Success

Another school of management literature suggests that managerial success is based on subordinate satisfaction and organizational commitment. The theory is that managers influence subordinate satisfaction and acceptance of organizational goals and values, which in turn influence work unit performance; this, in turn, will lead to the success of the manager. Evidence suggests that satisfied employees who are also committed and loyal to their organizational goals are more likely to be productive than employees who are dissatisfied and not committed to such goals. But the issue we would like to raise is whether manager *success* is indeed related to subordinate satisfaction and commitment. As the next chapter will clarify further, we did not find evidence to support such an assumption.

The Mythical Prescriptions for Manager Success

The adage instructs: "Keep your eye on the ball, your shoulder to the wheel, your nose to the grindstone, and your ear to the ground, and you will be successful." Could anyone really work in such a position? Which of these bits of sage advice are to be believed, and in what order?

The traditional management literature and classic theories lay down some specific guidelines to be a successful manager. For example, we noted in Chapter 2 that the "father" of the functional/process approach to management, Henri Fayol, prescribed a five-step approach to success: plan, organize, command, coordinate, and control. Other classical management theorists, such as Luther Gulick, recommended seven ingredients of success: plan, organize, staff, direct, coordinate, report, and budget. Other classical writers, such as Lyndall Urwick, have suggested as many as twenty-nine such ingredients. Every management function that has ever been conceived undoubtedly has a proponent somewhere.

If we consider all the prescriptions for manager success, we see that not very much is really known about the subject. Many of these traditional prescriptions appear to be only general guidelines, sometimes subject to serious error when they are followed. We found many successful departures from the classical prescriptions (for example, one successful manager came up through project engineering where most of the classical prescriptions were violated dramatically).

The traditional behavioral prescriptions involve such ingredients as team building, goal setting, coaching, facilitating and participating. These are merely representative and are generally implied rather than directly advocated for managerial success. There are obviously many other similar prescriptions that are thought to relate to manager success. We have examined more than 130 such factors in our literature search (which, as an act of kindness, we will omit here). We found that many of them relate to many things, but few relate to the success of the RMs we studied.

This chapter provides pragmatic advice and guidance for those who want to get ahead and climb the ladder of success in today's organizations. Networking and communication skills seem to be the most important keys to success. The next chapter comes full circle and answers the question of what do *effective* real managers do.

4 WHAT DO EFFECTIVE REAL MANAGERS DO?

After first attempting to answer the questions of what do real managers do (Chapter 2) and what do successful real managers do (Chapter 3), our analysis next turned to the third question of what do effective RMs do. This is the most important question because it represents the "bottom line" for the study of RMs—what do the most effective managers do? By the same token, it is the most difficult to answer because of the problems of defining effectiveness, trying to measure it in RMs in different organizations, and drawing general conclusions.

First, this chapter will present how effective managers have been portrayed in the traditional literature. Next, the difference between successful and effective managers will be emphasized. The balance of the chapter is devoted to the background and results of the third phase of the analysis that relates to the question of what effective real managers do.

THE TRADITIONAL PROFILE OF EFFECTIVE MANAGERS

Like the literature on activities of managers in general and successful managers in particular, much of the published information about effective managers and effective managing is prescriptive, given in "what to

Table 4-1.   Prescriptions for Effective Managers Drawn from the Literature.

---

1. Be proactive—initiate—anticipate
2. Control your time
3. Be the leader
4. Control your decisionmaking groups
5. Don't overcontrol
6. Don't undercontrol
7. Communicate
8. Don't get into trouble because of communicating too much
9. Keep your organization open with a high level of trust
10. Take time to reflect on problems and solutions
11. Seek help when you need it
12. Let the experts do their jobs
13. Be assertive
14. Renegotiate your job if you have to
15. Protect yourself
16. Choose appropriate objectives
17. Be accurate
18. Set realistic goals
19. Know the objectives
20. Choose the right people for effectiveness
21. Match jobs and people
22. Design your organization for effectiveness
23. Design the jobs for effectiveness
24. Create a supportive environment to get the job done
25. Encourage attitudes to improve productivity
26. Emphasize goals
27. Encourage action
28. Facilitate interaction among participants
29. Facilitate work
30. Be attentive to product quality
31. Arrange a clean, pleasant physical work environment
32. Develop yourself
33. Develop your subordinates
34. Motivate
35. Build up your subordinates
36. Make your subordinates want to come to work
37. Be patient
38. Be sincere
39. Recognize good work

Table 4-1. *(continued)*

---

40. Reward fairly
41. Don't demand performance from high performers
42. Do demand performance from low performers
43. Control poor work
44. Terminate non-workers
45. Properly deal with inspectors
46. Carefully build and control your budget
47. Keep good records
48. Participate in the community
49. Make it fun
50. Innovate—make positive changes

---

do," or worse, in "what to be" form. Managers reading the collection of "should-do," "should-be" prescriptions are sure to find that they are not following, and probably cannot follow, all of them.

Table 4-1 shows a representative sample of no fewer than fifty prescriptions for effective managers that we extracted from the considerable literature on the subject. Who can argue against these prescriptions? Most managers are trying, with varying results, to do these kinds of things, but no manager can effectively go in fifty or more directions at the same time. Are the prescriptions of equal importance? How much effort should be applied to what—and when?

Some RM activities take less effort and contribute more, or are more closely related to effectiveness measures, than others. If one were able to prioritize, or weigh these activities by order of importance, RMs then could better analyze their own strengths and weaknesses and systematically develop the most important activities first.

Later in this chapter, we will show the relative weight of the four activities of RMs (communication, human resource management, traditional management, and networking) identified in our study. We based our conclusions both on direct observation of RMs and on standardized questionnaires asking subordinates how they view the effectiveness of their managers. The intent here is not to urge RMs to do impression management (that is, managing impressions about their effectiveness) as a substitute for getting the job done or for such "hard measures" as quality, service, productivity rates, and profits. However, research methodologies with multiple sources (observers and subordinates in this case) along with perceptions and impressions of manager effectiveness have been demonstrated to be reliable and valid enough to draw some meaningful conclusions about what effective RMs do.

SUCCESSFUL VERSUS EFFECTIVE MANAGERS

"Successful" and "effective" are not interchangeable terms. In the literal sense, managers who are effective (those who have satisfied, committed subordinates and produce organizational results) are not necessarily those who succeed (those who are promoted relatively quickly). Anyone who has ever worked in an organization knows that such disparities exist and may have suspected that this was quite prevalent. Importantly, our study of RMs *empirically* found this to be the rule, rather than the exception. Successful RMs generally were not doing the same amount of the same activities as effective RMs.

Starting with the scientific management movement at the turn of the century, managerial effectiveness focused on getting the job done—in the most direct way. It mainly recommended a task-oriented approach as the key to effective management. Thus, organizational effectiveness stressing quantity and quality standards of performance was equated with managerial effectiveness. However, more recently, a more humanistic approach to management has also been advocated, at least in the literature. Thus, employee satisfaction and commitment have also become associated with managerial effectiveness.

Even though management practitioners, writers, researchers, and even lay people, tend to view successful managers and effective managers as the same, and use the terms "successful" and "effective" interchangeably, the difference may be vital to explaining the current state of American management. If indeed there is an empirically demonstrable difference between successful RMs and effective RMs, it could explain why American organizations are being outdone by foreign competition, and why U.S. productivity is growing at such a dismal rate. Perhaps even more critical is the growing frustration and deteriorating confidence that hard-working, effective RMs seem to be experiencing in recent times. One manager explained:

> It seems that no matter how hard I work, I can't seem to get ahead in this company. Sure, I get a pat on the back once in a while and I'm assured a secure position. But the smooth talkers, not the hard workers, seem to move into top management around here. Its very frustrating to me to work my tail

off on a project, involve my people and make sure it's done right, when I know it may not be as important as my golf game and being able to talk sports with the boss.

Analyzing effective RMs versus successful RMs has not been done in the literature to date. Yet, this important distinction between effectiveness and success may be crucial to the understanding and practice of modern management. Chapter 3 defined and analyzed success; now we will do the same for effectiveness.

HOW WE DEFINED MANAGERIAL EFFECTIVENESS

Measuring manager effectiveness, a seemingly simple task, can become hopelessly complex. Table 4–2 shows the representative areas identified in current references measuring managerial effectiveness or performance. As shown, there are almost 2,000 different measures that could be used for manager effectiveness.

Obviously, 2,000 or even 44 measures (the smallest number shown), are too many to evaluate in a study of manager effectiveness. Nevertheless,

Table 4–2. Sample Number of Available Measures of Manager Effectiveness.

1. Production	252
2. Sales	199
3. Comptroller	180
4. Marketing	172
5. Personnel	169
6. Facilities/Plant	144
7. Purchasing	125
8. Manufacturing/Industrial Engineering	102
9. Materials Handling	93
10. Maintenance	91
11. Production Planning	83
12. Treasurer	81
13. Research and Development	76
14. Quality Assurance	66
15. Data Processing/Management Information Systems	65
16. General Effectiveness	44
Total	1942

getting accurate and meaningful measures of both successful RMs and effective RMs, especially across organizations (in order to draw overall conclusions), must be attempted in order to answer the questions of the study of RMs empirically. In Chapter 3 we used an empirical definition of success, the managerial success index (MSI). As explained, the success measure was essentially a promotion index derived by dividing the level of managers by their tenure in the organization. In order to maximize control, to do sophisticated statistical analysis, and to determine if level or type of organization made a difference, the observational data on a sample of 52 RMs from a limited number of organizations were studied. Although we did do an effectiveness analysis of these same 52 RMs in order to make a direct comparison of successful versus effective RMs, this effectiveness part of the study also drew from a larger observational and questionnaire data base collected over the four-year period. To best answer the question of what do effective RMs do, we drew data from that collected by the participant observers on 178 RMs and questionnaire data from their direct subordinates. This sample came from a large number of organizations, from all types of industries (manufacturing, retail, service, transportation, financial, and public organizations).

To avoid the problems of a single measure of effectiveness, we used a combined, multiple measure containing three dimensions: (1) organizational unit effectiveness in terms of quantity and quality of performance, (2) subordinate satisfaction, and (3) subordinate organizational commitment. Standardized questionnaires (the Mott Organizational Effectiveness Questionnaire, the Job Diagnostic Index, and the Organizational Commitment Questionnaire; see Supplemental Readings and References for complete citations), all with high reliabilities generally and in this study in particular, filled out by subordinates, were used to measure the three dimensions of RM effectiveness.

To determine what effective RMs do, we first calculated the average or mean of the squared correlations between the observed activities of the RMs and the combined effectiveness measure (organizational unit effectiveness and subordinate satisfaction and commitment) as determined by their direct subordinates. We then ordered these correlation-squared means in terms of their relative strengths. This gave us the relative contribution of each of the four activities to RMs' effectiveness and gave what we believed was the best answer possible to the question of what do effective RMs do. To summarize, our effectiveness analysis took the following steps:

1. The correlations between RM observed behavioral categories (those listed in Table 2-1) and the effectiveness combined measure (unit effectiveness, subordinate satisfaction, and subordinate commitment) were squared. This was done to approximate variance explained.
2. These squared measures were averaged across samples.
3. Ratios were established between each observed RM behavior and the strongest related behavior (highest squared number) in the set (for example, the strongest was 1.00, one half as strong would receive 0.5).
4. These ratios were averaged across RM component behaviors that formed each of the four major activities (networking, traditional management, communicating, human resource management, as shown in Figure 2-1). For example, the traditional management activities are represented by the averaged ratios for controlling, planning, and decisionmaking behaviors. The ratios were averaged, rather than added, to preclude our influencing the contributions of the activities. If the ratios had been added, the activity with the highest number of component behaviors would have been the highest contributor to RM effectiveness.
5. The sum of the activities was represented as 100 percent of that contributing to effectiveness. The resulting pie charts (Figures 4-1 and 4-2) indicate the relative strength of each activity contributing to RM effectiveness.

One could, of course, argue with this approach in terms of either our measures of effectiveness or our use of correlational data (which, importantly, do *not* allow us to infer that these activities *cause* effectiveness) and relatively simple descriptive statistics. However, we would counter that multiple methods (observations and questionnaires) and multiple sources (RMs and their subordinates) were used in the study, and multiple measures (organizational unit effectiveness, satisfaction, and commitment) were used for effectiveness. In addition, we would defend our use of relatively simple correlational and descriptive statistics instead of more sophisticated inferential statistics, because it is our intent to *describe* what effective RMs do. We did another analysis using questionnaire scales (for example, scales from the Leader Behavior Description Questionnaire, Managerial Behavior Survey, and Job Diagnostic Survey), which conceptually related to the observed managerial activities, and found similar results. In other words, we had convergence between methods, in a large four-year study, to give confidence to our findings of what effective RMs do.

RESULTS OF THE EFFECTIVENESS ANALYSIS

To directly compare the successful RMs with effective RMs, we first used the same sample of fifty-two RMs used in the success analysis of Chapter 3. However, in this analysis only, the effectiveness measure combined subordinate satisfaction and commitment only; the organizational unit performance measure used in the rest of the analysis was not available to us on this sample of fifty-two RMs. The results are shown in Figure 4–1. Notice that there are some distinct differences between the relative contributions of the four RM activities to success and effectiveness (defined in this case as subordinate satisfaction and commitment) using the *same sample.* In particular, note the reversed roles of networking (strongest for success, weakest for effectiveness) and human resource management (second strongest for effectiveness, weakest for success). These differences between successful and effective RMs will be discussed further in this chapter and in the subsequent chapters that explore each of the activities in detail.

To do a more comprehensive, fully descriptive treatment of RM effectiveness, we went beyond the sample of 52 managers used in the success part of the study and analyzed 178 RMs and their direct subordinates (an average of about four subordinates each). We used the correlations between the directly observed behaviors of the 178 RMs' activities and the combined effectiveness measure, which included this time the organizational unit performance scale as well as the subordinate satisfaction and commitment scales. The relative strengths of the contributions of the four major activities to effectiveness are shown in Figure 4–2. Notice that these proportions of activities drawn from this large sample ($N = 178$ RMs) are almost identical to the smaller sample ($N = 52$ RMs) used in Figure 4–1. In other words, for both the small and large samples, the results were the same: networking had the strongest relative relationship with success and the weakest with effectiveness; and human resource management had a solid relationship with effectiveness (second strongest) and the weakest with success. Now let's take a closer look at each of the four major activities as they contribute to RMs' effectiveness.

Figure 4–1. Comparison of the Contributions of RM Activities to Effectiveness and Success (*N* = 52 RMs, using combined subordinate satisfaction and commitment measure of effectiveness).

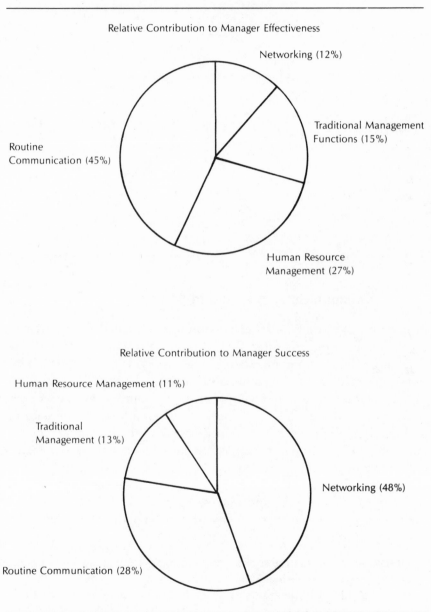

Relative Contribution to Manager Effectiveness

Networking (12%)

Traditional Management Functions (15%)

Routine Communication (45%)

Human Resource Management (27%)

Relative Contribution to Manager Success

Human Resource Management (11%)

Traditional Management (13%)

Networking (48%)

Routine Communication (28%)

Figure 4–2.   Contribution to Manager Effectiveness (N = 178 RMs, using combined effectiveness measure of organizational unit performance and subordinate satisfaction and commitment).

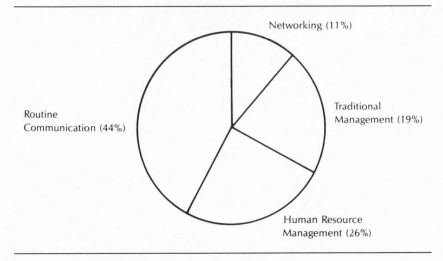

Networking (11%)

Routine
Communication (44%)

Traditional
Management (19%)

Human Resource
Management (26%)

Communication Activities of Effective RMs

Not surprisingly, we found that communication related to effectiveness more strongly than any other RM activity. This was true of both exchanging routine information behaviors (answering routine procedural questions, receiving and disseminating requested information, conveying the results of meetings, giving or receiving routine information over the phone, and attending staff meetings of an informational nature) and handling paperwork behaviors (processing mail; reading reports; emptying the in-box; writing reports, memos, and letters; routine financial reporting and bookkeeping; and general desk work). In fact, exchanging routine information had the highest relative strength of relationship to effectiveness, and processing paperwork had the second highest of all the managerial behaviors observed in the study. One manager commented:

> I'll have to admit that the secret to getting things done in my department, and keeping my people happy, is simply to keep them informed. I constantly get on the phone to them or stop by their desks to tell them or ask them what's going on. I also keep up with my paperwork and meet all my report deadlines

Because the communication activity was so strongly related to RM effectiveness, we also analyzed *how* RMs communicate. We asked a sample of 120 RMs from a small number of diverse organizations to fill out a questionnaire reporting their communication behaviors. Figure 4–3 shows that almost half of their self-reported communication was with subordinates. The remainder was distributed among others outside the organization (about one-fourth), others inside the organization (about one-fifth), and least with their bosses (about 15 percent). In addition, they reported, by far, that most of their communication was on an informal face-to-face basis, rather than via telephone, scheduled meetings, or written memos. Chapter 6 will discuss communication activities in considerable detail.

Human Resource Activities of Effective RMs

The activity second in its relative contribution to RM effectiveness was human resource management. Much of today's literature, for both researchers and practitioners, deals with the importance of human resource and humanistic approaches to management. However, the practitioner-oriented literature usually supports its cases with intuition while the

Figure 4–3. Those with Whom RMs Communicate (*N* = 120 RMs, using a self-report questionnaire).[a]

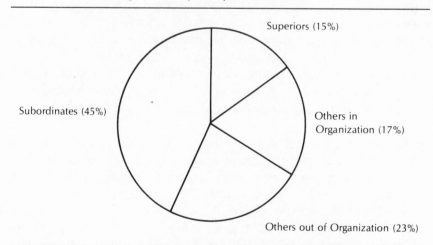

Superiors (15%)

Subordinates (45%)

Others in Organization (17%)

Others out of Organization (23%)

[a]Adapted from Fred Luthans and Janet K. Larsen, "How Managers Really Communicate," *Human Relations* 39, no. 2 (February 1986):167.

research-oriented literature relies on questionnaire survey results or unrealistic laboratory results. Our observational study verified the assumed importance of human resource management activities for the effective performance of RMs. One manager elaborated:

> I know how to handle my people. I don't let things fester. When any of my people have a grievance, they know that we can settle it together. They know where they stand, and what I expect. I take a hard line on bickering—just don't tolerate it, but I always recognize and reward good work. I make sure that everyone who works for me knows his job. We operate like a big family in my department. I have good people working for me—and I back them to the hilt. They know I care, but I'm not a busybody or a "softy." Once in a great while, I have someone who can't carry responsibility for his own work. Then I have to replace him. I don't like it, but in the long run, it saves me and everyone else in the department a lot of grief. Caring about my people "works." These guys really produce when you need them.

Importantly, this study found a measured strong relationship between human resource management activities and RM effectiveness. As noted in Chapter 2, human resource management activities include four categories of observable behaviors. Managing conflict (resolving interpersonal conflict among subordinates or others; appealing to higher authority or to third-party negotiators to resolve a dispute; trying to get cooperation or consensus among conflicting parties; and attempting to resolve conflicts between subordinates and oneself) had the strongest relationship with effectiveness. Following closely were staffing behaviors (developing job descriptions for position openings; reviewing applications; interviewing applicants; hiring; informing applicants of hiring decisions; and "filling in" where needed), and training/developing behaviors (orienting employees; arranging training seminars; clarifying roles, duties, and job descriptions; coaching, mentoring, doing task walk-throughs; and helping subordinates with personal development plans). Motivating/reinforcing (allocating formal organizational rewards; soliciting input/participation; conveying appreciation and compliments; giving due credit; listening to suggestions; giving positive performance feedback; increasing job challenge; delegating responsibility and authority; letting subordinates determine how to do their own work; sticking up for the group to superiors and others; and backing a subordinate) had a slightly lower relationship with effectiveness.

These human resource management behaviors are more personalized than the ones associated with traditional management activities.

Their strong relationship to effectiveness empirically demonstrates that the human resources approach seems to contribute greatly to RM effectiveness. Also, importantly, the observable behaviors that make up these activities clearly illustrate that such a human-oriented approach does not erode the RMs' formal power and authority to get the job done. On the contrary, RMs can strengthen and increase their bases of power using a human resources approach and reap the results on the "bottom line." Chapter 8 is devoted to these human resource management activities.

Traditional Management Activities of Effective RMs

The traditional management activities ranked third out of four in the relative contribution to RMs' effectiveness. As discussed in Chapter 2, the traditional management activities consist of the basic functional behaviors of decisionmaking, planning, and controlling. The controlling behaviors (inspecting work; walking around; monitoring performance data such as computer printouts, production, or financial reports; and doing preventive maintenance) related more to effectiveness than did the other two. Close behind, however, were planning behaviors, such as setting goals and objectives; defining necessary tasks to accomplish goals; scheduling employees and making timetables; assigning tasks and giving routine instructions; coordinating activities of different subordinates and groups to keep work running smoothly; and organizing the work. Weaker in relation to RM effectiveness were the decisionmaking behaviors of defining problems; choosing between two or more alternatives or strategies; handling day-to-day operational crises as they arise; weighing trade-offs and doing cost/benefit analysis; developing new procedures to increase efficiency; and actually deciding what to do.

The finding that decisionmaking has the relatively weakest relationship with effectiveness is most interesting because American business education tends to emphasize, and even equate good management with, decisionmaking. It may be that today's organizations, with emphasis on strategic decisionmaking, have moved this function exclusively to the top levels and have left out the typical RM. The planning and controlling behaviors remain relevant to RMs, but most (at least formal) decisionmaking has moved steadily upward in American business organizations. This observation is consistent with some of our interviews and interactions with RMs. One manager said:

> The key to doing well and getting the job done around here is to be organized and to stay on top of things. Staying on top of things is a full-time job. For example, we're just getting computers on-line in some of our major service areas. They'll help us to organize and control our work better and give us more time for long-range planning and innovation. Up till now, only the front office has had computer capabilities, so we had to rely on them to do our planning and controlling for us down here. They made all of the decisions and we had to implement them. We hope that is now going to change.

Chapter 5 will discuss the traditional management activities in depth.

Networking Activities of Effective RMs

The networking activities of RMs had the weakest relationship to effectiveness. This, of course, is in stark contrast to its relationship to successful RMs where it had—by far—the strongest relationship. Of the two component behavioral categories that make up networking, the "interacting with outsiders" behaviors (doing public relations; contacting customers, suppliers, and vendors; attending external meetings; and doing community service activities) were more strongly related to effectiveness than "socializing/politicking" behaviors (network related chit-chat; talking about family or personal matters; informal "joking around"; discussing rumors, hearsay, and the grapevine; complaining, griping, and downgrading others; and politicking and gamesmanship).

The findings of the success and effectiveness analyses seem to indicate that RMs' networking activities are a way to get ahead in an organization, to be successful, but have little to do with the contribution to effectiveness of RMs. These findings would support the notion that those RMs who are being promoted (that is, are successful) are good at and pay a lot of attention to social and political skills, but are not necessarily the most effective. Effective RMs are those who give relatively more attention to the other activities, especially communicating and human resource management. Once again, however, definitive conclusions must be tempered by the definitions of the terms involved and the analysis techniques used.

Chapter 7 is specifically devoted to this important, but seemingly complex and overlooked managerial activity.

EXPLODING THE MYTHS OF MANAGERIAL EFFECTIVENESS

The fifty prescriptions and the approximately 2,000 available measures of managerial effectiveness mentioned at the beginning of this chapter are a managerial puzzle that needs to be reduced to basics. The prescriptions in Table 4–1 all focused on ways for the RM to control specific results. We defined RM effectiveness in terms of influencing others in their environments (subordinates, peers, bosses) in order to get their jobs done. This involves earning the trust of the people they must influence. Trust connotes a reputation for predictability and fairness—a difficult goal at best, an impossible one for the non-communicative, non-human-oriented manager. This is precisely what our observations of RMs show: the most effective RMs do more communicating and human resource management activities than those who are less effective.

How does this "explode" myths of managerial effectiveness? When Henri Fayol laid down his principles of management in the early part of this century, the economic, legal, and cultural environments favored the manager. Although his freedom was shrinking, he still had the power to run his organization like a feudal barony (some managers still do). He could employ at will. He could freely set working hours, compensation, and performance standards. Although standards for sheer physical effort (long working hours, heavy lifting, and so forth) were higher than they are today, overall productivity was low by today's standards (mechanized, automated production was still in its infancy). The environment external to the organization was more stable. Consequently the organization, the work, and manager/worker expectations changed slowly. The world—markets, organizations, jobs, tasks, and expectations regarding pay, promotion, and treatment—is now far more dynamic. Although these changes don't signal the fall of traditional approaches to management, they do herald a need to reexamine *how* managers implement those traditional approaches. When we find something that "works," we stay with it—often to the exclusion of something else.

Take *planning*, for example. It is common for RMs trained as functional specialists (for example, accounting, finance, operations research, or even personnel) and working in their specialities (as technicians) during their formative years as managers, to identify their success with this technical aspect of their career. The result is that when they move into positions involving more interaction with subordinates, they will probably retain the habits of concentration and the need for isolation and privacy that were essential in their earlier technical experiences (and successes).

The same can be said for the *organizing* function. This area usually focuses on organizing data, events, materials, and processes, and structuring the organization. Here again, specialists can progress early in their careers, oblivious to the many implications their work has for trust, subordinate commitment and satisfactions, and, most importantly, the effects they can and do have on their people and the effectiveness of the unit.

In the *staffing* function RMs are often confronted with a "Catch-22." No one wants to reward weak performers or overlook strong performers. Nevertheless, RMs in the staffing function often do just that. They allocate more resources to the weakest performers. The weakest performers receive extra training, extra attention, and occasionally even extra rewards (particularly when performance is impossible to measure objectively or when "improvement in performance" measures are used). At best, many personnel systems simply fail to distinguish performance differences through recognition and reward systems. We were amazed at the number of experienced RMs who, over time, develop a blind spot to this issue.

An exemplary case is the organization of 300 employees with a performance recognition program founded on one "employee of the month" for the entire organization (the likelihood of being recognized is less than once in twenty-five years). A second such case was a large organization with serious performance problems and high waste rates, involving complex processes with new technology. Their product is unusually sensitive to the quality of worker input. When asked what options were available to recognize differential performance, the RM responded with, "They get their paychecks." With more than twenty years of field experience, this manager is a product of the traditional management school. He's honest and dedicated to hard work. His subordinates, with experiences different from his own, have different performance-reward expectations.

Some elements of these upside-down reward systems are unavoidable. But differential rewards based on differential performance in the long run become necessary for effective performance. Pursued on the basis of technical adequacy, without regard to their effects on subordinate attitudes and performance, traditional prescriptions for managerial effectiveness are myths. Traditional management principles remain important. But the catalyst that translates these from myth to reality is at the core of RM effectiveness. RM effectiveness resides in considering the effects of traditional management processes on worker trust in the organization through predictability (the workers' ability to predict their outcomes based on their own performance), training and developing, motivating/reinforcing, and results in unit performance and subordinate satisfaction and commitment. This doesn't imply that communication and human resource management are the only ingredients of effectiveness. It does suggest that for the most effective RMs communicating and human resource management activities are an *integral part* of organizational effectiveness. Those less effective deal with the human component by fragmenting it, often leaving it to other functional specialists and technicians.

A FINAL WORD

In many ways, the question asked in this chapter—what do effective RMs do—is the most important in the whole book. The last chapter on successful RMs is important for those managers looking for pragmatic ways to get ahead in organizations—keys to success, if you will. But for the "success" of today's *organizations*—pragmatic ways for them to move ahead in terms of increased productivity and outdoing the competition (both foreign and domestic)—the key is the *effectiveness* of their managers. We found that effective management (as defined by subordinate perceptions of organizational unit performance, both quantity and quality, and subordinate satisfaction and commitment) is most strongly related to communicating and human resource management activities. Obviously, it would be nice if we also had "hard" measures of effectiveness, such as profits, costs, and service. Because these were impossible to obtain in our type of comprehensive study across diverse organizations, we feel as confident as possible in answering the question posed in the chapter title: effective RMs do relatively more communicating and human resource management activities.

5 TRADITIONAL MANAGEMENT ACTIVITIES

THE EMPIRICAL BACKDROP

Although traditional management activities account for approximately one-third of what all managers do, our analysis of successful and effective managers showed that these activities did *not* fare well. Among successful real managers, for example, traditional management activities were near the bottom; only human resource management had a weaker relationship. Among *effective* real managers, only networking had a weaker relationship. In short, our study, unlike the widely publicized results of Mintzberg's observational study of five CEOs, found RMs doing traditional management activities, but both successful and effective RMs gave them little attention, as Figure 5–1 illustrates.

In our study, traditional management activities were defined as the observable behaviors associated with *planning* (setting goals and objectives, defining and assigning tasks, scheduling, setting up timetables, giving routine instructions, coordinating activities, and organizing the work); *decisionmaking* (defining problems, choosing between alternatives, handling day-to-day operational crises, weighing trade-offs, conducting cost/benefit analyses, developing new procedures, and actually deciding what to do); and *controlling* (inspecting the work, walking around, monitoring performance data such as computer printouts and

Figure 5-1. Distribution of Traditional Management Activities.

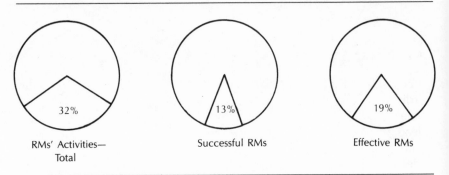

32%	13%	19%
RMs' Activities— Total	Successful RMs	Effective RMs

production and financial reports, and doing preventive maintenance). Table 5–1 provides some actual examples of these activities derived from our interviews. The following sections examine each of these major categories of the traditional management activities—planning, decision-making, and controlling—in more depth. In this and subsequent chapters we begin to blend our empirical findings on RMs outlined in Chapters 2, 3, and 4 with the literature and theory of management. We draw primarily from our considerable experience with the RMs, based on qualitative data and personal interactions, to support a point in the discussion, rather than use systematically gathered participant observation and structured interview and questionnaire data, as we did in Chapters 2, 3, and 4.

PLANNING

Planning, a widely recognized traditional management activity, was found to be a major activity of RMs. Management literature generally defines planning as the process of setting objectives and then determining the steps needed to attain them. The first step in this process typically involves scanning the environment to identify opportunities. At this time the organization will determine those things that it should do or stop doing. Quite often, forecasting is used at this stage of the planning activity to focus on such areas as new product or service development, sales, technological breakthroughs, and changes in the sociopolitical environment.

Table 5-1. Traditional Management Activities: Some Specific Examples Drawn from Structured Interviews.

	Planning	
High Amount	*Medium Amount*	*Low Amount*
Meets with sub-ordinates and sets objectives and deadlines, reviews dates and gives specific instructions necessary to attain these goals.	Sets objectives with subordinates and re-mains available to answer questions re-garding the plan.	Informs subor-dinates of their assigned objec-tives and the date for their com-pletion.

	Decisionmaking	
High Amount	*Medium Amount*	*Low Amount*
Examines all the facts related to a problem and dis-cusses the situation with those in-volved before making a decision.	Discusses the situation with others and then delegates the matter to knowledgeable sub-ordinates.	Briefly reviews the situation and makes an expe-dient decision.

	Controlling	
High Amount	*Medium Amount*	*Low Amount*
Makes personal visits, on both a scheduled and an unscheduled basis, to check on the work performance of subordinates and to determine those problems that need to be considered.	Uses formal reports and informal meetings as the basis for deter-mining how well things are going in the unit or department.	Follows up and controls situations that have gone unresolved and now need per-sonal attention in order to correct them.

The second step in planning is the establishment of goals or objectives. At the upper levels of organizations, this generally consists of determining overall strategic goals such as return on investment, growth of market share, and operational objectives such as profit, productivity, and quality control. At the lower levels, the focus is on day-to-day concerns, with operational objectives receiving primary attention. These include such things as work assignments, sales quotas, cost control, and productivity standards.

The third step of the planning process deals with determining and choosing alternative courses of action. Having set objectives, the enterprise will now decide how to attain them by giving subordinates specific tasks to perform and ensuring that these activities are coordinated to maximize work output.

The fourth step involves following up and ensuring that everything is done in accordance with the plan. This step blends planning into controlling, thus providing a feedback loop for additional planning. It also shows the interrelationships between the traditional management activities of planning, decisionmaking, and controlling.

Our study revealed a number of specific behavioral activities that RMs were directly observed to do while carrying out the planning process. The following examines some of the most important of these.

Setting Goals and Objectives

Real managers set goals and objectives for their people, sometimes unilaterally, sometimes as a mutual process involving give-and-take on both sides. In particular, we discovered RMs devoting a great deal of attention to ensuring that goals were clear, understandable, and in harmony with those of the overall unit. One RM described the process this way:

> My job is to carry out the assignments given to me by the boss. These assignments have to be broken down into smaller goals that can then be divided up among my people. If I do this right, then we're all moving in the same general direction—both me and my group. The first place to begin is to figure out what the overall objectives are that I've got to accomplish. How is my boss going to evaluate my performance? The answer to this is the basis for goal-setting in my unit.

Defining Tasks

The definition of tasks is a natural adjunct to goal-setting. At this point, the manager decides what specific things need to be done. The process basically involves breaking overall goals down into subgoals. One manager explained:

> My sales region is in the midwestern part of the U.S. There are five states in this region. On the one hand, it's not too difficult to define the task—it's to get out there and sell. On the other hand, this is a very general description of what needs to be done. The people in the field need a lot of support help, and I have to ensure that the salespeople get this support. So when I start defining the overall tasks for this group, I have to take into account sales and nonsales activities alike. A lot of this is based on experience. In the beginning, my planning was poor because I didn't consider all of the tasks involved in selling. However, after eight quarters of sales feedback, I pretty much know what I'm doing. All I really have to find out from corporate is what my total sales quota is. I can take it down to my people from there.

Scheduling and Assigning Work

Having determined the specific objectives of the unit, RMs next focus on scheduling the work for their people. This involves reviewing what everyone in the group does, and determining their capabilities and availability. This is then followed by assigning work to each person. Quite often, the latter task is not very difficult. Most people tend to specialize or work in a specific functional area such as sales, advertising, quality control, or personnel recruiting. The manager's job is to match the work to be done with the individual's expertise. However, sometimes it is not this easy.

Some people may be working on a project or task that is not yet completed and are thus unavailable for any additional assignments. Others may want to expand their abilities and be assigned something outside their area of current expertise. Of those remaining, none may have the requisite training or experience to do the job properly. One RM commented:

> I find that once people learn their jobs, they often like to move on to other, more challenging assignments. This means that I'm continually throwing

people in over their heads—they either lack the training or the experience to do the work efficiently. On the other hand, this is what makes the work so interesting and enjoyable around here, and it's a problem that I've just had to learn to live with.

RMs are challenged to be aware of how much work everyone in the unit is expected to do. We found that some RMs assigned difficult tasks to those who do the best job without considering that these people often end up doing more work than anyone else in the unit. Conversely, those who do not work effectively were given very little to do because the manager did not want to take a chance on their performance. One manager tried to balance the work loads so that everyone ended up doing their fair share:

> Most people in my department do a good job and I have no complaints with their work. However, I look at more than the amount of work they do. I also look at quality. It's easy to get bogged down for days on a complex, five-page cost control report while someone else is processing 500 orders a day. The two jobs don't equate in terms of quantity. The first person looks as if he isn't doing much of anything, while the second one is working furiously. I keep my eye on these things by noting the difficulty of the tasks that I assign to people. I've learned that there are two types of work overload: quantitative and qualitative. I can see the first one—all I have to do is go by the person's office and look at how much work is piled up on the desk. I can't see the second one, but it's there. Usually, it involves "think" work that takes strenuous mental effort. No one can be subjected to a great deal of qualitative overload without finally wearing down. That's why I try to balance the work loads so no one gets too much of it.

A third major challenge related to assigning tasks involves clarity and expectations. When people are given tasks that are unclear to them, they will not carry them out in the desired manner. There are a number of ways to prevent this type of breakdown. One of the most effective is to make sure subordinates know what they are supposed to do *before* beginning the job. This means asking subordinates *what* they are going to do and having them explain the steps that they will take. Then, if there is a problem, the RM could prevent the mistake by correcting the subordinate's plan of action and substituting a more effective one. Here is one RM's example:

> One of my people recently went out West to give a sales pitch to a new client. One of the things we stress to our people is the importance of punctuality. If you're late arriving for the meeting, the client will think you don't want the business. If your presentation runs too long, the client feels that you

haven't thought it all through very well. Because I was going to be in the area, I made it a point to accompany him to the meeting. At 9 a.m. sharp, we were ready to begin. However, the head man of the client company hadn't arrived yet. My sales rep didn't know what to do. He leaned over and asked me and I told him to hold up everything until the CEO got there. The CEO arrived five minutes later, apologized for his tardiness, and we were off and running. If I hadn't been there to tell my rep to wait, he'd have started without the president and we probably would have lost the sale. Sometimes, no matter how hard you try, people will carry out their tasks incorrectly. That's why I really go out of my way to urge people to ask questions if they are unsure of what to do.

Coordinating the Work

Coordination is the synchronization of effort between employees. In many jobs, coordination is vital to effective performance. This is as true for office work as it is for assembly line operations. In fact, any project or job that involves a committee or team of people is likely to have coordination requirements. The manager's job is to ensure that the personnel involved in the project coordinate their activities so that they are moving in unison as a team.

We found that RMs used a number of procedures to promote coordination. One was to make all involved parties aware of the fact that they have to coordinate their activities. A second way, particularly useful when a group or project approach is being used, was to help plan formal time periods during which the members come together, discuss their progress, and talk about how they should proceeed. A third was for the RM to get involved, if only on a periodic basis, by talking to the subordinates, discussing their group efforts, pinpointing any coordination problems they were having, and helping resolve these situations. A fourth was to review periodically what everyone was doing to ensure that all were in step with one another. One manager elaborated:

> One of the biggest problems with coordination is that most people have been brought up to do things by themselves. That's the American way. However, in this business, it's a team effort that produces the best results. There can't be one or two big stars; there have to be a lot of "no-name" team players. In ensuring coordination throughout my unit, I make it a point to check on progress two to three times a week. If there's a problem, I want to know about it and start working to resolve it right away. Coordination often involves soothing a lot of egos: when one person is hurt or angry over something and

decides not to cooperate with the others, everyone ends up with the problem. I see my job as that of a facilitator who helps coordinate things and keeps the process moving along.

Organizing the Work

Organizing is more than just the organization chart; it also involves assigning and delegating duties to subordinates in order to ensure maximum efficiency. Much of what has already been discussed is part of the organizing process. However, organizing also involves ensuring that everyone knows who reports to them and to whom they report. Additionally, it calls for formally giving people the authority they need to get the job done. One RM commented:

> When I assign one of my people a task to do, I tell them what I want done and by when. At the same time, I let them know what authority they have. In this way, they understand the limits within which they are operating. There's no sense giving someone a job and then undermining his authority by letting his staff come directly to me for advice, counsel or orders. There's a chain of command around here. I respect it and I expect other people to do the same.

DECISIONMAKING

Decisionmaking, the second traditional management activity, is the process of choosing between alternatives. There are a number of ways decisionmaking is carried out. On a formal basis, RMs examine financial data, read reports, and gather additional information on a particular problem or project. Then, having reviewed the data and interpreted the material in as much depth as time allows, they make their decision. On an informal, more realistic basis, the manager gathers as much pertinent information as quickly as possible. Depending on the nature of the issue, the individual may spend anywhere from one minute to a couple of hours on the matter. Then, having analyzed the available information, the RM makes a decision.

Most textbooks present decisionmaking in terms of managers making detailed analyses of situations, gathering extensive amounts of information, and drawing conclusions based on formal decisionmaking techniques, such as operations research or other quantitative tools. In truth, most RMs are confronted with situations that require much less sophistication—and even if it were required, many would avoid using unfamiliar mathematical tools and techniques. More commonly, RMs gather whatever information they can quickly amass, use logic, intuition, and experience to help them analyze the data, and then make a decision.

The literature on managerial decisionmaking suggests three characteristics relevant to our study of RM activities: simplicity, probability assignment, and rationalization. Simplicity refers to the fact that RMs tend to make quick decisions and do not spend a great deal of time analyzing complex data. In fact, once "enough" information has been acquired, most RMs seem to reject any additional input as overkill. Once they feel they have sufficient information to make a decision, they do so. Moreover, if new information were suddenly uncovered that showed previous data to be erroneous or incomplete, and this new development would require them to start the decision analysis all over again, RMs are likely to reject the new information. Having made a decision, RMs are not interested in further analysis; they want to move ahead with the decision process.

The assignment of probabilities involves the likelihood of a particular event occurring. Most RMs do not formally assign probabilities. As a result, they tend to overrate the likelihood of rare events and underrate the likelihood of common events. When RMs are unfamiliar with decisionmaking situations, they typically err in assigning probabilities to the expected outcomes.

A typical example is found among firms that insist that their managers purchase flight insurance at the airport. Statistics show that this insurance is extremely expensive given the likelihood of an airplane crash. It would be wiser for the firm to abandon this policy or use the funds that are spent annually on flight insurance to purchase additional health or term insurance for their executives.

Rationalization is the ability to defend decisions in the face of criticism. Many RMs make decisions they feel will stand up to scrutiny rather than those that they feel will provide the greatest payoff to the organization. In doing so, they often gather data that supports their choice or shows why one of the other options is a poor one. If their decision is questioned, they are able to defend the choice.

The above three characteristics (simplicity, probability assignment, and rationalization), influence and modify the decisionmaking activity of RMs. In carrying out this process, there are several more specific activities that we found RMs undertaking. The following sections discuss these and give representative examples.

Examining the Problem

Most RMs approach decisionmaking by getting feedback on the problem or issue and using this to help them identify the cause. Depending on the nature of the problem, this part of the decisionmaking process can extend anywhere from a few minutes to a couple of hours. Most situations are not particularly time consuming. They usually involve talking to subordinates or others who have information related to the issue or reviewing material that provides background data. Examples range from investigating the reason for a drop in sales in a geographic region, to gathering information related to why someone was fired for fighting in the workplace, to evaluating the benefits associated with installing computer workstations throughout the company. One manager told this story:

> My sales group was number one in our region last year. However, the only way to move up the ladder in this firm is to work your way into the largest sales region in the country and then make the move to upper level management. A year ago, my turn came and I was given the western region. That's the good news. The bad news is that sales here had fallen while all of our competitors were growing. I was not only surprised to learn what had been going on, but also I didn't have the foggiest idea of how to deal with it. However, I thought the best thing to do would be to get some background information and see if I could pinpoint a possible cause. After going through our sales and personnel files for hours, I came across the reason. It seems that we were growing so fast in the West, we were hiring and putting people in the field who had no experience or training in sales. I reversed this and sales have definitely improved.

Making a Cost/Benefit Analysis

There are a number of ways to make a cost/benefit analysis. The easiest way is to compare the costs of the various decision alternatives against their payoffs; the one with the best ratio then is chosen. RMs in our study however, usually found it too time consuming and expensive to approach anything but the most important decisions in this manner. In most cases, they would work with just a few alternatives and base the cost/benefit analysis on whatever data could be gathered in a timely manner. Sometimes financial or other forms of computerized data were available; other times the comparison was highly qualitative in nature.

An example of a quantitative approach to cost/benefit analysis is the following case:

> We were working on various alternatives for improving our office productivity. One of the primary areas of consideration was computerization. We decided to find out how efficient it would be to set up workstations and train our people in how to use them. I started out by having a couple of major computer companies look over our operation and then give us written proposals covering costs and expected work output. I knew that their costs were somewhat negotiable, so I knocked 10 percent off these figures. I also knew that their efficiency estimates would be too high, so I knocked 20 percent off these. I then used the results to put together a series of cost/benefit analyses.

An example of a qualitative approach to cost/benefit analysis is the following:

> We were invited to make a product presentation to a new company. If we got their business, it would mean a big jump in our annual sales and a hefty bonus for all of us on the sales team. However, I just wasn't sure how to make the presentation. We didn't know anything about the management of this firm or the type of presentation that would be most effective. I didn't even know if the competition had also been invited to give their pitch. In any event, after thinking the matter through very carefully, I decided that it would be best to focus the presentation on the practical aspects of our product and how it would save them money. If I was going to make a mistake, I figured it would be best to err on the conservative side. We later learned that one other company made a presentation and that it was viewed as all flash with no substance. We got the contract from them a few days after the presentation. My gut instinct really paid off.

Developing New Efficiency Procedures

Another specific decisionmaking activity of RMs is that of developing new efficiency procedures. This activity typically involves studying situations to determine how things can be done faster or less expensively. The range of alternatives included here is quite extensive. Common examples include: developing cost reporting systems that help pinpoint problem areas; reorganizing work routines to improve coordination and reduce bottlenecks; and creating (and sometimes serving on) commit-tees that investigate operations and explore efficiency shortcuts. The objective of these procedures is to reduce costs and increase bottom-line performance. Here are some additional representative descriptions. One manager discussed inventories in this way:

> We started looking into ways to reduce our cost per unit. I thought it would be useful if we examined the feasibility of using a just-in-time inventory tech-nique. I mentioned the idea to three of our suppliers and found that they would implement the idea if we paid for any additional out-of-pocket ex-penses that they had, such as transportation and warehousing. We agreed with the transportation expenses, but the warehousing costs were what we were trying to eliminate altogether, so we started looking at ways that we could coordinate our efforts to ensure that the suppliers could also keep their inventories to a minimum. It took six months but we did it. Today, our inventory costs are way below what they used to be.

Another RM covered sales expenses:

> We have almost a hundred salespeople on the road at all times and we reim-burse their expenses, within certain limits, of course. I began looking at how much it cost us to process all of these reimbursement claims, using considerable office help. I then talked the president into giving everyone a company-owned credit card to cover all of their expenses. Now, all of the bills come directly from the credit card company to one person who checks them out. If anyone has gone overboard on his expenses, an agreed-upon amount is deducted directly from his paycheck.

One RM talked about work flow:

> We used to have six people assembling our small, hand-held appliances. Each would do part of the assembly and then pass it on to the next person. I changed the assembly configuration by having each worker assemble an entire unit. The time we saved by not passing units from one worker to an-other more than offset the loss of efficiency created by one person having to perform all of the tasks. Today, our output is a little higher than it was under the old assembly arrangement and the workers seem to take more pride in their work because our reject rate has dropped.

Handling Operational Crises

RM decisionmaking includes handling operational crises that can take a number of different forms. One of the most common is dealing with situations that require rapid decisionmaking. In most cases, this type of crisis occurs without warning and has to be handled as quickly as possible. Common examples include: equipment failures or breakdowns; correcting major safety violations that constitute a threat to the safety of employees; a rash of quality flaws or defects; running out of inventories or supplies; and initiating counterstrategies to meet competitive price efforts to take business away from the company. One manager elaborated:

> I was just getting ready to leave the office late one Friday afternoon when I got a call from one of our regional managers. He had an early copy of the Saturday paper and it contained an ad announcing a major sale by our biggest competitor in this region. The weekend is our biggest sales time of the week. We couldn't let this strategy go unchallenged. It took me a few hours to reach my boss and get an approval to meet the price. I then called back the regional manager and told him that all of our stores were to meet the competitive price. We, of course, didn't get an ad in the paper, but we did put signs outside every store announcing our new low prices. The result was that I'm sure the competition didn't do half as well as they anticipated. However, it took some fast decisionmaking to prevent us from being snookered by the competition.

Choosing between Alternatives

Choosing between alternatives is the essence of decisionmaking. On a formal, rational basis, cost/benefit analysis can be used. Whether this is carried out on a quantitative or qualitative basis, the RM identifies the "best" alternative and then implements it. However, as was pointed out earlier, sometimes the formal, rational approach (such as cost/benefit analysis) is a myth in RM decisionmaking. In some instances, outside factors enter the decision process and either resurrect a rejected alternative or create a new one, which is then chosen for implementation. Here are two representative examples:

> A couple of months ago, I was asked to conduct a cost/benefit analysis related to purchasing personal computers for our office. After looking over the information, it turned out that [name of company] had the best product for the money. However, when I told my boss about the decision, he disagreed. 'I want a company that's going to give us first-class service and that's IBM. Buy what you want, but if it's not IBM, you better not have any trouble with the equipment.' Last week, I put in an order for several personal computers from IBM.

We had spent the better part of two months examining different approaches to handling our training and development needs. I contacted a local university and talked to their Executive Development Institute. We agreed on a price for conducting a series of ongoing management seminars. However, at the last minute, we got funding in the budget for in-house facilities and we brought the entire program in-house. Until that funding came along, however, we had no idea that it was a feasible alternative and hadn't given it any serious consideration.

CONTROLLING

The third and final major traditional management activity identified in our study was controlling. The literature defines this function as the process of evaluating results and taking action in light of the findings. Controlling is a natural follow-up to the planning and decisionmaking activities. After defining objectives (planning) and deciding how to implement the objectives (decisionmaking), the RM next must determine how well things have gone and what, if anything, to do in light of the findings. There are a number of specific behaviors that RMs were directly observed to do in controlling operations. The following sections examine some of these major controlling activities.

Inspecting the Work

Inspecting involves making proactive, prescheduled checks on subordinate or work group performance. This can take a number of different forms. One is weekly meetings at which progress is discussed, roadblocks are identified, and action plans are formulated. One manager explained:

> We have a staff meeting every Friday morning from 9–10 a.m. At this time, we examine our quality control record for the last five operating days and talk about what problems we're having. Once we've identified them, we discuss how to deal with them. Now, an hour isn't a lot of time to identify problem areas and decide what to do, but if you can do this every week, it's possible to stay on top of the quality control area. Thanks to these meetings, we've cut the quality reject rate considerably.

Management by Walking Around

Management by walking around (MBWA) was popularized by Thomas J. Peters and Robert H. Waterman, Jr. in their best-seller, *In Search of*

Excellence. They found that managers in the excellent firms used this approach. Instead of staying behind their closed doors and working at their desks, the managers from the "excellent firms" got out with the personnel, walked around, asked questions, got first-hand information, and used face-to-face communication to learn what the problems were and how to resolve them. We found that RMs make wide use of this technique of control. One manager learned the value of MBWA this way:

> I used to spend a lot of time taking care of my work at the home office. I figured if one of my managers had a problem, he could call me up or come by and talk to me. Otherwise, I didn't want to get in my managers' way by always being out in the field snooping around. However, about six months after I started managing this sales region, we began to have a lot of problems between our suppliers and our stores. This showed up in the form of lower sales per store caused by stockouts. At first, I didn't pay a lot of attention to it. After three or four weeks, however, I thought I better get out there and find out what was causing the problem. I'm glad I did. The story I got from the store managers was totally different from what the suppliers told me, but one thing was certain—it couldn't go on. We got it resolved within forty-eight hours and ever since then I've made it a point to spend at least one day a week walking around out there and finding out how things are going. A passive approach to control is okay, but it's got to be supplemented by face-to-face control. Since I've started this practice, I've never had another problem like this one.

Another manager values MBWA for this reason:

> I always make it a point to get out of my office and walk around. I want to know what's going on outside the office, how people are doing, what problems they've got, what I can do to help them do their job better, what rumors are floating around. The result: there is virtually nothing that happens around here that I don't know about. Last month, a rumor got started that there was going to be a cutback in our work force. I checked the rumor out with top management, found it to be untrue , and made sure the word got out that it wasn't true.

Monitoring Performance

Monitoring of performance can take many different forms. Inspecting and MBWA are two of them. Other common ways this is done include: monthly cost control reports; sales results; forecast and performance comparison data; tardiness, absenteeism, and turnover reports; and production or output data. All of these generally compare feedback with predetermined objectives. Based on the results, action is then taken. This action also can take a number of different forms.

If the objectives are not attained, the RM will want to determine why and decide if some changes are in order. These can be as simple as a reduction of 10 percent in the next quarterly sales forecast or as drastic as a cutback of 25 percent in the sales force, coupled with scrapping a major product line that is not selling. The range of possibilities is extensive. Two real managers gave the following examples:

> Our quarterly sales results were right on target. Everything looked fine. However, as we examined the computer printouts in more detail, it became obvious that we were doing a lot better in the rural areas than we had anticipated, but were not doing well in the urban areas. We were having a great deal of trouble developing a niche in the face of competition from major retail chains. On the other hand, in areas where competition was soft, we easily dominated. Based on that data, we began building all of our new stores in towns of 50,000 or less. As a result of that decision, we now have a dynamic annual growth rate.

> Our production objective was 2,700 units a day. However, after fourteen months, we were still unable to reach this objective. We started out at 1,800 a day and worked our way up to 2,200 a day, but seemed unable to move any higher. I then began reviewing the feedback information and eventually realized that the problem was not that output was too low, but that the number of personnel was too high. We had more people than we needed and they were getting into each other's way. I reorganized the work assignments and transferred a number of the people to other areas. Within three months, we were up to 2,500 units a day.

Doing Preventive Maintenance

The preventive maintenance activity involves taking proactive, corrective action before a piece of equipment breaks down or a system needs adjustment. This often is referred to as feed-forward control. It involves making adjustments before things go wrong. There are a number of ways that this process can be used. Here are two examples:

> We used to do preventive maintenance on our machinery on an "as-required basis." However, after studying the production records, I realized that it would be a lot cheaper to schedule maintenance on a periodic basis. We decided to institute this practice on machinery in Section 4. The results showed that our downtime was greatly reduced and our costs of maintenance

also went down. Because we scheduled the maintenance to fit the availability of the repair crews, we were able to keep them busy at all times rather than having them working at a frantic pace when a handful of machines suddenly went down, and then sitting around doing nothing when all of the machines were up and running. Preventive maintenance has been one of the biggest control measures we introduced around here.

We used to send people to training and development seminars whenever their bosses indicated that they needed it. I changed all of this six months ago by showing my managers that training and development should be given before our people needed it, not after they have indicated that they have a deficiency. Result: our people are now better equipped to do their jobs and we are generating more and better work with the same number of people.

A FINAL WORD

RMs do perform the traditional management activities of planning, decisionmaking, and controlling. However, it is important to realize that RMs do not spend nearly as much time on these activities as management textbook writers over the years have indicated. Also, both successful and effective RMs give relatively little attention to these traditional activities. Nevertheless, the traditional management activities of planning, decision making and controlling are still important. By studying how the RMs do them, we can learn a lot about managers and managing in today's organizations.

6 COMMUNICATION ACTIVITIES

THE EMPIRICAL BACKDROP

Almost a third of the observed activities of RMs were routine communication. Only the traditional management activities were observed slightly more often in the RMs studied. Among successful managers, communication activities showed about the same relative contribution, but they were, by far, the major relative contribution to effective RMs. The top third of successful RMs did about 10 percent more of this activity than the bottom third (see Chapter 3). The relationship of the communication activities to RM effectiveness was far stronger (44 percent) than any other activity (see Chapter 4). As Figure 6–1 illustrates, RMs do a lot of communicating activities; the successful ones, and especially the effective ones, do relatively more.

Communication is the process of transmitting meanings from sender to receiver. This process is well known and respected by management educators and trainers as well as by real managers. It is generally recognized that the communication process consists of five elements: a sender, the message to be transmitted, the medium used to carry the message, the receiver of the message, and the interpretation given to the message by the receiver. As defined in our study of RMs, the communication activity involved two basic categories of observable behavior:

Figure 6–1.   Distribution of Communication Activities.

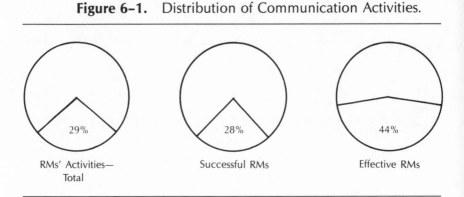

| RMs' Activities— Total | Successful RMs | Effective RMs |

exchanging routine information (answering procedural questions, receiving and disseminating requested information, conveying the results of meetings, giving or receiving routine information over the phone, and holding staff meetings of an informational nature) and *handling paper work* (processing mail; reading and writing routine reports, memos and letters; doing routine financial reporting and bookkeeping; and carrying out general desk work). Table 6–1 provides examples from our interviews of how both of these activities were actually carried out by RMs on a day-to-day basis.

This chapter first examines the communication flows in real organizations, then discusses the major barriers that RMs face in communicating. The last part of the chapter provides some specific guidelines for increasing communication effectiveness. The discussion blends the empirical findings from our study of RMs with management theory and literature. The supporting RM comments are representative of our experience with them over the four years of the study.

COMMUNICATION FLOWS

There are a number of ways in which communication flows in real organizations, including downward, upward, laterally and diagonally. We found each form used by RMs both to convey and receive routine information. Table 6–2 shows the distribution of these flows as reported by a sample of our RMs. As shown, most of the communication reported by RMs was to their subordinates in the downward flow and from their subordinates in the upward flow. Relatively less communication occurred

Table 6–1.   Routine Communication Activities: Some Specific Examples Drawn from Structured Interviews.

Exchanging Routine Information		
High Amount	*Medium Amount*	*Low Amount*
Has a formally scheduled meeting with all departmental personnel on a weekly basis to review cost control data and pinpoint problem areas.	Makes it a point to visit with all of the departmental personnel and pass on to them the latest ideas that are conveyed at the monthly managerial meetings.	Posts information that is sent down from higher level management on the employee bulletin board for all to see and read.

Handling Paperwork		
High Amount	*Medium Amount*	*Low Amount*
Makes sure that all cost control reports are completed on time and submitted to the central office in triplicate.	Reads all of the incoming correspondence and sees that any information that should be forwarded to other personnel is done so immediately.	Makes sure that all memos are reviewed and initialed before sent out under his or her signature.

from or to their superiors. Also, both the downward and upward flows, as reported by the RMs, took place verbally (face-to-face, over the phone, or in meetings), rather than in written form.

Downward Communication

Downward communication travels from superior to subordinate. The two most common reasons for this type of communication flow are: to provide instructions and job-related information directly connected with carrying out tasks; and to provide subordinates with general information related to the organization and unit at large. There are many different types of downward channels, including memos, face-to-face

Table 6–2. RM Self-reported Communication Flows in Five Diverse Organizations (N = 120).[a]

	Downward		Upward	
Types of Communication	To Subordinates	From Superiors	From Subordinates	To Superiors
Mean frequency per week	48.7	13.9	50.6	17.7
Percent face-to-face	83.4	76.9	81.1	82.4
Percent telephone calls	10.2	11.4	9.8	12.8
Percent meetings	13.8	19.6	9.0	12.6
Mean frequency of memos per week	3.7	3.2	3.4	2.3

[a]Adapted from Fred Luthans and Janet K. Larsen, "How Managers Really Communicate," *Human Relations* 39, no. 2 (February 1986): 168.

conversations, public address systems, bulletin boards, and in-house newspapers.

The primary advantage of downward communication is that it provides direction and control for the employees. However, there can be a number of problems associated with downward communication. For example, verbal information expands as it moves down the line. Simple messages take on additional meanings as they travel from one level to the next. Only a small percentage of all messages that are passed through hierarchical levels emerge in their original form. Most have been greatly expanded through reinterpretation. One manager faced the issue this way:

> I know that when information is passed down the line, people like to add their own ideas and interpretations to what is being communicated. I can't stop this. However, during my weekly staff meetings, I put aside a short time at the end to discuss policy changes and other information that has come from the top. I try to get feedback from my staff on what this means to them. If there are any misinterpretations or rumors that need to be handled, I do it then. I can't guarantee that my people are going to always believe what I tell them, but at least I know how they are interpreting all the information that comes down from above.

When messages must move through more than one level, it is best to put them in writing. Additionally, any information that is considered to be important should be put in writing if only to have a record of what was "really" communicated. However, most managerial communication literature points out that whenever possible, written communication should be supplemented by oral communication. It is felt that the subordinate needs to get the message twice. The written statement provides a constant reference that can be consulted if clarification is needed; the oral discussion provides a refinement of those points that are not clearly spelled out in the written communication. One manager does this two-step communication with his staff:

> Whenever I have a meeting with any of my subordinates and we agree on some new work assignment, I always do two things. First, I make sure they know exactly what they are supposed to be doing. Second, I follow up our meeting by sending them a memo. In this way, if there has been a miscommunication, they can get back to me. At the same time, I have a record of what we agreed on so if there is a problem later on, I can dig out the memo and review it with them. I find this approach works really well. My boss uses it with me and I use it with my people.

Upward Communication

Upward communication involves messages that flow from subordinate to superior. The most common purpose of upward communication flow is to provide feedback on how things are going. This flow seems to be particularly important in gauging how well subordinates understand what is going on, how well they are carrying out their tasks, and in creating the esprit de corps vital to high quality work. As Table 6–2 shows, the most common type of upward communication flow by far is face-to-face. However, written communiqués are also used, especially when subordinates want to have a formal record of something that they conveyed to the boss.

The primary advantage of upward communication is that it gives the subordinates an opportunity to convey their point of view on various matters. It also gives RMs feedback on how well things are going so they can identify emerging problems before they become serious.

Similar to downward flows, there are a number of problems associated with upward communication. For example, whereas downward verbal communication expands, verbal information contracts as it goes up the line. This seems particularly true when bad news is communicated. For example, we found that when a subordinate would tell an RM something negative or unpleasant (for example, "Salaries are way out of line given the relative amount of work people in this department do."), this statement was likely couched in a much milder, briefer message (for example, "Salaries need to be raised.") In other words, if there is a large amount of verbal information being passed up the line, the bad news tended to be distorted or filtered, while the good news arrived almost intact. Written communiqués flowing upward tended to be read, remembered, and acted upon based on the degree of brevity, the ease with which the RM could implement or make a decision on them, and the benefits that such decisions offered to the people involved. One manager recognized this tendency:

> I insist on getting important information from my subordinates in writing. The everyday things can be verbal. However, either way, I bet that I'm not getting the whole story. My people love to blow good news my way while sweeping bad news under the rug. I've found there's only one way to overcome this habit. I keep my ears open and if I hear some disturbing news through the grapevine I let my subordinates know about it. I can't run an effective department if people don't tell me everything—good and bad. I think I've been using the grapevine since I took this job and I believe that all the other effective managers in the company do, too.

Lateral and Diagonal Communication

The third type of communication flow is lateral and diagonal. Lateral communication takes place between managers who are on the same level of the hierarchy. The most common reason for this type of information transfer is to promote teamwork and coordination. One manager explained:

> If we're going to get things done around here, we have to know what the right hand and the left hand are doing. Keeping in close touch with the other departments often helps cut through red tape and helps me network throughout the company. It's important to know what's going on around you to keep everyone going in the same direction.

Diagonal communication, on the other hand, which takes place between RMs who are not in the same department or on the same level of the hierarchy, can be slightly up or slightly down.

These two forms of cross communication are not as widely used for routine communications as they are in networking activities (see Chapter 7). Nevertheless, RMs use them to convey general information. Because they involve people outside the manager's direct sphere of operation, these communication flows can create problems. One of the most common is that their use can be interpreted as a power play. One example would be: "What's Chuck, from quality control, doing talking to Mary, from computer operations? I'll bet he's trying to get some information about the latest quality control reports before they're made available to the productivity committee."

Whether or not such interpretations are true, lateral and diagonal communications can be the basis for rumors that carry erroneous, and sometimes potentially harmful, information. To minimize the possible problems associated with cross communication, the following guidelines found in the literature and generally supported by our effective RMs were formulated:

1. One's immediate boss should be consulted, if only informally, before formally communicating across departmental lines. In this way, the boss knows what is going on and can shield the manager from unwarranted criticism.

2. The boss should be kept informed of any significant results that occur because of the cross communication. For example, interdepartmental arrangements that call for representatives from each department to coordinate their efforts may result in better performance for all departments involved. However, unless the respective superiors know what is going on, they may feel that the RM in question has gone beyond his or her authority. Additionally, any interdepartmental arrangement that benefits one side more than the other is likely to draw the wrath of the boss whose side is being shortchanged. By ensuring that no such arrangements are made without the full understanding and consent of the superior, RMs protect themselves from the backlash that is likely to follow an agreement that has unfair advantages.

3. Unless there is good reason to keep things verbal, memos should be exchanged between the parties involved in lateral or diagonal communications that result in new work assignments or other job-related changes. This ensures that each party is aware of what is going on.

DEALING WITH COMMUNICATION BARRIERS

Regardless of which type of communication flow is involved, it is common to find various barriers that prevent the free and complete transfer of meanings between sender and receiver. We found that many RMs were aware of these barriers and knew useful ways to deal with them. The following examines some of the most prevalent barriers and provides some representative ways to overcome them.

Perceptual Barriers

Perception is a person's interpretation of reality. Since no two people have ever had exactly the same background experiences in life, no two perceive things exactly the same way. Everyone, including RMs, look at the world through their own perceptual glasses.

Empirical reality is the objects, events, and behaviors that people observe. Perception, in turn, interprets these objects, events, and behaviors to give them meaning for the person. Sometimes, empirical reality and interpretive perception overlap and empirical reality can help the interpretation. One example would be a manager who sees his boss and another department head loudly exchanging words. The reality is that the RM sees two people who are standing close to each other and yelling about something. From an interpretive standpoint, the RM perceives the two as disagreeing over some matter and expressing their anger in the form of loud arguing. Consider another example. A manager receives a memo from the boss which says that effective immediately all overtime is cancelled and will not be reinstated until the company works down its large backlog of inventory. This is the empirical reality. However, the RM perceives this to mean that if sales do not pick up in the very near future, the company will start laying people off. Empirical reality, the typed memo, set the stage for interpretive perception, expanding (interpreting) the words that were in the memo outside the realm of that message.

Of all the possible causes of communication breakdown, perceptual problems are perhaps the most common. In dealing with such perceptual problems the literature suggests, and our effective RMs generally would support, the following:

1.   People tend to interpret reality to suit themselves. Thus, whether something is in written or verbal form, receivers will tend to modify

the message mentally so that it fits their view of reality—or what they would like reality to be.

2. To understand the perception a subordinate has of a particular message, a real manager has to know that person's background. For example, during hard economic times, union members are likely to interpret cost-saving needs as a prelude to wage concessions or even terminations. When management secures a new, large, government contract and announces that it will start hiring in the near future, many of those who have been looking for overtime will interpret this announcement to mean that management will only hire to fill the production gap not addressed through overtime work.

3. Perception tends to be defensive and protective in nature. People performing below expectations are more likely to perceive this failure to be a result of external conditions (for example, lack of effort from supporting personnel, poor equipment, or inadequate training provided by the company) rather than of internal conditions (for example, poor personal work habits, lack of skill, or low motivation). Any management pronouncements related to "getting rid of dead wood" are typically interpreted to mean that other people's jobs are at stake but not their own.

4. Verbal communications are more likely to result in perceptual problems than are written communications. People tend to remember those parts of a verbal message that are in agreement with their own position and downplay or forget those parts that conflict with their position. Therefore, verbal messages have a higher likelihood of suffering perceptual adjustment; listeners alter or change the message to suit their point of view. A representative example of this problem is the following:

> A few months ago, I convinced my boss that we should allocate at least some money for merit and not have our usual across-the-board raises. However, I made a big mistake. I told my best worker what was about to happen and that he could look forward to a hefty raise. Unfortunately, by the time he told everyone else, the story was completely changed. According to the latest rumor I've heard, there are to be no more automatic raises—only merit raises. That's not what I told him! I did manage to save the day, however, by putting out a memo that spelled out exactly how raises would be handled in the future. Now all I have to do is hope my boss doesn't find out that I'm the one who leaked the initial story to a talkative subordinate.

5. Written communiqués are more useful than verbal ones in reducing message distortion because there is less opportunity to translate or

freely interpret what is being communicated. A well-written message typically results in far less distortion than a well-spoken message.

Inference Barriers

An inference is an assumption made by the receiver of a message. Just as empirical reality and perception can overlap, so can inference and perception. When a message is unclear or ambiguous, receivers will draw inferences that are in line with their own way of thinking. However, such inferences can become problems. Particularly in written communiqués, any part of a message that is unclear will call for an assumption to fill in "between the lines." The greater the number of inferences required, the more likely it is that the sender's intended meaning will not be the same as the receiver's interpreted meaning. In dealing with inference problems, the literature suggests that our effective RMs would support using the following guidelines:

1. Written messages need to be as self-explanatory as possible. To ensure that they are, the sender should allow for some time between the writing of the message and its conveyance. This gives the sender time to reread the material and ensure that it is as clear as possible.
2. When possible, the sender should have important written communiqués checked by others (for example, trusted associates) to ensure that the directive or policy is clear to them. If it is not, their questions or suggestions should be noted and the communiqué should be rewritten to address these concerns or ambiguities.
3. In verbal communication, there should be time for feedback from receivers (for example, answering questions or addressing concerns). This feedback allows the manager to explain the message and deal with objections or problems that, if not handled now, will crop up later. Nonverbal cues (especially facial expressions) can also be helpful feedback in this regard.

The importance of answering questions and providing feedback is made particularly clear by the following story:

We had a memo come down from the top brass a few months ago. It related to the new layoff policy and whoever wrote it must have copied it directly out of the union-management contract without adding any explanation. The essence of the memo was that in case of a layoff, those who were hired last would be dropped first. However, there was nothing about the fact that those with seniority in other departments could return to their old units and bump people there who had less seniority than they did. The memo wasn't incorrect, but it was incomplete. We almost had a riot on our hands. Whoever wrote the memo should have clarified the fact that the message related only to intradepartmental policy regarding layoffs. Better yet, he should have added a section on bumping. In any event, it was necessary for the top management and the top union officials to follow up with another memo to explain the rights of those who were laid off in a particular department. What you don't tell people seems to cause as many problems as what you do tell them.

Language Barriers

Language involves the structure of words that are used in a message. These words can become a barrier to communication when the receiver is either unfamiliar with them or misinterprets their meaning. For example, in many organizations the word "burn" is used to mean "photocopy." Unless new employees are made familiar with the jargon of the trade, the individual who is told to "burn this original set of blueprints" is likely to destroy the materials. Similarly, new salespeople who are told that they are required to attend bimonthly staff meetings at the home office may take half a day to come to the office two weeks later, only to find that the meetings are every two months and not twice a month.

The first of these two examples is more significant because: unless the receiver is aware that there is a language problem, the individual will not take any corrective action until after the mistake has been made; and the problem is not restricted to the organization itself—new suppliers, customers, clients, and others who come into contact with the organization are likely to be subjected to this trade jargon and to respond incorrectly to it.

In overcoming language barriers, the literature suggests and our effective RMs would support the following guidelines:

1. As part of the socialization process, all new organization members, as well as key outsiders, should be made aware of the specialized jargon. This is particularly important when a word or phrase has a totally different meaning than it does in general practice.

2. All new or key outside people should be encouraged to ask questions related to operations and procedures. If the RM in charge does not have the time or knowledge to answer all of them, an experienced subordinate or knowledgeable person should be assigned to the newcomer or outsider to handle this function.
3. Keep in mind that meanings are not in words, they are in people. The way people interpret a word dictates what that word means to them. For example, telling a subordinate to "get this report completed as soon as possible" may result in the person dropping whatever he is doing and focusing exclusively on the report. This same message may be interpreted by another subordinate to mean that when she has finished with the financial data analysis she is running, she could begin work on the report. Adding a clarifying statement can avoid such problems.

Here is a representative way of how the language problem is effectively handled:

> In my department, I make it a point to talk to all of my new people the first day they're on the job. Then I schedule another meeting with them during their third or fourth week. During this session, I try to find out how well they have learned the ropes, the jargon, the informal rules, and everything else they ought to know. It's all right to be naive when you first come in here, but I expect this to be overcome within a couple of weeks. If it isn't, I want to know why. Sometimes there are things that the new hire still hasn't been told or hasn't learned. In other cases, he is just too slow and has to be told again. In any case, I want this problem solved—and fast. It's the only way to bring new people up to speed and prevent a disaster around here.

Status Barriers

Status refers to the relative ranking of an individual in a group, organization, or society. Especially in organizational settings, status becomes extremely important because it lends credibility to those in higher level positions. CEOs tend to be more believable because of their position than department heads. Similarly, at least in the eyes of top management, a supervisor is more credible than a worker. Status problems occur when *who* people are is given greater weight than *what* they are saying or the evidence that supports their point of view.

In dealing with status as a communication barrier, the literature suggests and effective RMs would verify the following guidelines:

1. In conveying information, the communicator's status often influences the message's credibility. This can result in blind acceptance or rejection of messages. In order to discourage such action, it is important for RMs to foster honest, open feedback. Status problems can be minimized if RMs let subordinates know that they want to be given accurate information and if they reward those who do so.
2. Both knowledge and experience influence the accuracy of communication. When RMs have these two qualifications, their status becomes a minor issue. RMs who "have the facts" are often regarded as more credible than higher status managers who lack such knowledge.

The following representative story tells how an effective RM would deal with status problems:

> When I hold small meetings in my office, I make it a point to deemphasize my position in the company. I don't think you can be effective unless everyone feels equal. I try to create this type of environment by gathering everyone around a large round table that I have in my office. I get out from behind my desk and sit with my people. Now, this doesn't guarantee that status won't be a problem, but I think it is a way of minimizing it.

EFFECTIVE COMMUNICATION ACTIVITIES OF RMs

The communication activities of real managers were identified in the study as the observable behaviors associated with exchanging routine information and processing paperwork. These observable behaviors, of course, are not as exotic or sophisticated as the terms and supposed functions presented in the traditional managerial communication literature. Nevertheless, the identified RM communication activities still encompass basically the same processes and dimensions as have been discussed and analyzed over the years. A review of these will lead to a better understanding of how RMs communicate and what they do to improve the effectiveness of communication.

Understanding the Communication Process of RMs

When people communicate, there are four generally recognized steps involved: attention, understanding, acceptance, and action. The literature suggests, and the effective RMs would support, the conclusion that unless all four of these steps are carried out, there is a good chance that the communication will break down.

Attention.   Attention is attained when the sender is able to get the receiver to focus on the message and to screen out all disturbances and distractions that can interrupt the necessary concentration. This means overcoming message competition. There are a number of things that can be done to help secure such attention. Two of the most helpful are these:

1.   Start off with an attention-getter. For example, one of the RMs told us that when he gave a presentation to the finance committee asking for more funding, he would always present what the main competitor was doing in this area of the business. Because the competitor's funds were usually greater, he could always get the committee's attention.
2.   Focus on something that is of primary importance to the receiver. If the receiver is interested in trimming expenses, gear the communiqué to those steps that will help reduce costs. If productivity is a major concern, explain how the plan will lower the cost per unit of production.

Understanding.   Understanding requires comprehension on the part of the receiver. The biggest problem here is that while most RMs realize the importance of achieving understanding, they often fail to get it. Why? If they think the receiver does not comprehend their message, they ask the receiver, "Do you understand what I've just said (or written to you)?" Receivers almost always say, "Yes." All the pressure is on the receiver to do so, particularly in the case of downward communication. Few RMs are going to admit to their boss, "I lost you about five seconds into what you were saying." Instead of asking receivers if they understand, senders should ask *what* they understand. This gives receivers a chance to put the message into their own words; and if they are incorrect the sender can say, "No, that's not what I meant to convey. Here's what I'm trying to say." Again, when senders are finished, they should ask receivers to restate the message.

Acceptance.   Acceptance occurs when the receiver is willing to go along with the message. Quite often this compliance is automatic; the RM may ask a subordinate to do something and the individual does it. However, sometimes there is resistance which, if not picked up by the sender, results in communication failures. For example, the subordinate may already be overburdened with work and unable to drop everything to find a particular report that has been mislaid. At other times, subordinates may feel that they lack the proper training to carry out the task. For example, the subordinate might say, "I don't know anything about printing files using that word processing program. However, if it can wait until after lunch, Bob will be back and he can take care of it." However, if the RM pushes and says, "There's nothing to it. Get in there and try it, you'll get the hang of it almost immediately," the manager is refusing to acknowledge the subordinate's lack of acceptance. Sometimes this is a good idea because it forces people to train themselves in jobs that they might not voluntarily undertake; at other times, however, the RM is making a mistake by pushing the matter. One manager made this distinction:

> I generally have people respond very quickly to me, but I may not get the results I want. When I tell them something, I emphasize two things: what needs to be done and what type of assistance or support will be provided. Look, if I ask someone to fill out the montly cost control report and he's never done it before, he's not going to be very receptive to my comments about this being good training. In fact, he thinks he's being dumped on. What I try to do is provide him with previous reports, call in someone who has done these reports before and have this expert brief him on what to do. Then I make myself available to answer questions or get additional assistance if he needs it. People don't mind going the extra mile for you if they think you'll be there for them if they run into trouble.

In dealing with acceptance, the literature suggests and effective RMs would verify the importance of the following:

1. Feedback (both verbal and nonverbal) from the receiver is important. If the individual is given an order or directive and is not allowed to say anything about it, acceptance can only be inferred. If there is a problem, it will not show up until the work is either late or incorrectly done. Communication feedback should not only be tolerated, it should be encouraged.

2. If it is important that the subordinates do what is being asked, the effective RM does not take no for an answer. Effective managers get subordinates the training or assistance needed, and give them moral support and the coaching necessary for the job. However,

they also must get subordinates to accept the order by using effective persuasion. Effective RMs rely on threats or disciplinary punishment only when all else fails.

The Importance of Simple, Repetitive Language

The simpler a message, the more likely it will be understood and acted upon properly. Simplicity takes two forms: direct and complete. Direct means that the message gets to the point without providing information that is supplementary, tangential, or simply filler. Complete means that when the message has been relayed, the listener understands everything that the communicator wanted understood.

Simple messages should not be so brief that they leave out salient facts. Repetitiveness is also an important factor when the message contains a series of important facts or analytical or quantitative data that are difficult to digest. By repeating or restating these important facts, the sender increases the likelihood of the message being fully comprehended. The literature suggests, and effective RMs would support, the following guidelines:

1. Do not belabor the point. Determine what is to be said and say it. If the communiqué contains bad news, the effective RM would prepare the other person for it by making introductory remarks that explain the reason for the news. For example, if there is to be a layoff and the individual is to be one of those let go, the effective RM would start off by saying that economic conditions have made the action necessary and that some good people will have to be laid off. Then, after telling the individual that he or she is included in this group, the RM would point out the types of assistance the firm is going to provide or the letter of recommendation that the individual can expect. The remarks would be kept brief and the other person would be given a chance to talk. If nothing else, the individual will probably want to let off steam.

2. Remember that simple words always have greater communication power than sophisticated words. Although there is always the possibility of talking down to listeners, it is far more common for RMs to confuse them by using words that they do not understand than by using words that are below their level of understanding.

3. If a message contains a number of important ideas, it helps to repeat the major points as one goes along or recap them at the end. This

may seem trite but it will generally result in improved communication effectiveness. Although this may make RMs feel that they are talking down to their listeners, most of them will welcome repetition of important ideas because it helps them keep track of what is being said. Effective RMs know that every message should be understood. If the subject matter is complex, it should be communicated in manageable portions, giving listeners the opportunity to ask questions or seek clarification. Additionally, if RMs recap the message as they go along, listeners will find it much easier to follow the flow of information.

The Importance of Empathizing

Empathy means putting oneself in another person's place. In so doing, effective RMs begin to see things the way their superiors and subordinates do. By empathizing they can begin to know when to be work centered and when to be people centered. They are also capable of answering such questions as: what type of direction does this subordinate need?

The literature suggests that empathy is of particular importance at two stages of the communication process: acceptance and action. When a manager gives an order that a subordinate is reluctant to accept, the effective RM notices the subordinate's hesitancy through such nonverbal cues as facial expressions. For whatever reason, the subordinate may not understand how important the matter is or how significant his or her role will be. Empathy helps the RM determine the best way in which to communicate this importance and helps implement the action stage. The empathetic RM stays alert for signs that the subordinate needs assistance and then sees that this assistance is provided.

The literature emphasizes two major points about empathy with which effective RMs would agree:

1. Empathy is a result of understanding people's needs. Empathy can be improved by allowing subordinates the chance to communicate upward and by interacting with them on a continuous basis. In this way effective RMs begin to obtain improved insights into how their people feel about issues and what can be done to manage them more effectively.
2. There is a big difference between being empathetic and being a pushover. Effective RMs do not lose sight of the fact that their job is

to improve performance and obtain objectives. Empathy can help, but it does not mean that the manager should acquiesce to the employees' every need and desire. Effective RMs know that they sometimes must ask their people to do things that are difficult or unpleasant. However, the effective RM's first responsibility is to get things done, not to keep subordinates happy.

Here is a representative example of an RM using empathy:

I try to get to know my people so I know what's important to them. When I have to assign work, I know when to be flexible and when to push hard. Let me give you an example. Last month, the wife of one of our employees had a baby. The fellow was scheduled to go on a trip to the West Coast the following week. He called from the hospital, gave me the news, and asked if he could postpone the trip. It wasn't necessary—when I checked the assignment calendar earlier, I knew that his wife would be having the baby at about the same time he was scheduled to be out of town, so I had a replacement ready to move in. All it took was a little forward planning. Once I know what's important to my people in terms of their career development and personal life, I try to adjust the job to reflect this. The result is usually a win-win situation for my people, me, and—I know this sounds hokey—for the company.

The Importance of Understanding Body Language

Body language is one of the most important forms of nonverbal communication. This "silent" language takes many different forms—from posture to eye movement, to where a person stands in a room in relation to others. Although everybody uses body language, many are unaware that they do. There is considerable literature on guidelines for using nonverbal communication, and effective RMs are aware of the following:

1. Looking people directly in the eye is often, but not always, a sign of honesty. Good liars are able to look people right in the eye with no compunction. If anything, they have come to realize that eye contact is important to convincing their audience.

2. By looking people in the eye it is possible to get some idea of how much stress they are enduring. For example, when right-handed people are trying to deal with an issue on an emotional level, they tend to look to their left. The reverse is true for left-handed people.

3. Touch is an important way of conveying confidence, trust, or friendship. For example, a firm handshake is often regarded as a sign of self-assurance. Touching also is used to convey power relationships. For example, a manager who wants to emphasize an order may grasp the subordinate's arm while issuing the order. An RM who wants to give positive attention to a subordinate may put a hand on his shoulder. These forms of touching reinforce the RM's message.

4. Physical location can also help convey messages. For example, where the RM sits or stands in a room in relation to the subordinate may dictate the style and tenor of the message. When giving commands, RMs can convey greater authority if they stand up and the subordinate remains seated. This enables the RM to look down at the subordinate as the reprimand is delivered. When an RM wants to establish authority in the office, the furniture layout can help convey the necessary power. For example, by placing the desk as far away from the entrance door as possible RMs can increase their perceived authority—distance typically is equated with power. Other ways an RM can enhance authority include: keeping all visitors on the other side of the desk, using the desk as a wall between RMs and visitors; and placing the desk directly in front of a window so that visitors look into the sunlight while RMs have the sun behind their back. On the other hand, if a manager wants to convey a friendly image, he may come out from behind the desk and sit on the opposite side with visitors. This eliminates the desk as a barrier and quickly establishes a warm, open environment.

5. Even clothing can be used to convey messages. For example, some literature on the topic suggests that the most authoritative pattern for men is the dark, pinstripe suit. This is followed, in order, by the solid, the chalk stripe, and the plaid. For women in business, a conservative, tailored suit carries more authority than a more fashionable suit.

The Importance of Giving and Getting Feedback

Giving and getting feedback is perhaps the primary way for effective RMs to communicate. All of the communication barriers discussed earlier can be overcome with effective feedback. There are a number of ways in which this can be done. One is by soliciting feedback from subordinates. While this can take numerous forms, some of the most effective openers include these:

- "Can you tell me more about . . .?"
- "You've given me some things to think about. I'd welcome any additional ideas you might have along these lines."
- "I think that we're ready to begin implementation of this project. What do you think?"

Each of these openers encourages subordinates to expand on their earlier comments or to voice an opinion regarding what to do now. RMs know that effective feedback depends on making the other party feel free to comment and that their input is valued. One of the best ways to ensure this is to keep the tone positive, as one manager attested:

> When I'm trying to give or get feedback, I follow one simple rule: make the other guy look good. I emphasize the positive rather than the negative. I never say, "How come things in your unit are all screwed up?" That's not going to get me anywhere. Instead, I review the positive aspects up to this point and ask how I can help the person get back on track if things are not going too well. I approach these matters by making it clear that we're all in this together. You'd be surprised how much people will open up when they find that your objective is to help them rather than catch them doing something wrong.

A second important aspect of feedback is sustaining the flow of information. For example, once the RM has subordinates talking, it is helpful to keep them going. This requires the use of phrases or statements that sustain the action. Some of the most useful are:

- "I understand what you're saying. But tell me, what else do you think we need to do?"
- "Right, right. This all makes a lot of sense. Keep going."
- "What else?"
- "I appreciate what you're saying. It's right in line with the way we've been thinking about approaching this problem. However, how would you handle the implementation phase of this idea? Whom would you include? How long would it take to get this all carried out? Give me more details on the specifics of your approach."

A third important part of feedback is giving the listeners additional information that elaborates or clarifies what has already been said. Some

RMs, fearing overkill, may be reluctant to do this because they think that their people already understand what has been communicated. In other cases, RMs may assume that if subordinates wanted more information they would ask for it. Actually, many subordinates are reluctant to solicit information from their boss for fear of appearing unqualified to do their job. As a result, they remain silent.

To sidestep this reluctance to ask questions, the RM can provide feedback without being asked to do so. The approach of effective RMs was to preface the feedback with an introductory question that allowed the subordinates to say, "No, I already understand that. It's not necessary to go on." A second way was to use an introductory remark that was congratulatory in tone, while at the same time, giving feedback on the matter. Here are some representative examples:

- "I read your report and think that it covers all of the important areas that need to be addressed. However, I'd like to share with you a couple of ideas for expanding it and incorporating more of the cost-related data."
- "I read your report very closely. I like it. What sets it apart from the others I've gone through is . . ."
- "Your progress on this subject has brought you to the point where we need to determine your next step. I'd like to give you my ideas on how we should proceed."

In each of these scenarios, the manager approached the feedback from the standpoint of the receiver. Each comment conveyed something of help or value to the receiver and encouraged him to listen to what is about to be communicated.

The Importance of Developing Effective Listening Skills

Of all the communication activities carried out by RMs, listening may be the most overlooked. Here are listening skills that are suggested in the literature and that effective RMs have developed:

1. Listen to what is being said rather than how it is being said. This means that instead of dismissing the speaker as boring or uninteresting, the effective RM lets the person speak and focuses on the message.

2. Give the speakers a chance to convey their message: hear the person out. It is also important for the listener to assume that the other person has something important to say. In this way, the listener focuses attention more closely.

3. Encourage speakers to stay on the main topic by asking them pertinent questions that redirect them back to the subject.

4. Fight the tendency to tune the speaker out when the presentation becomes overly technical or too difficult to understand. Focus on listening, learning, and remembering.

5. Watch the speaker's approach and see what can be learned. For example, in a formal presentation, did the person effectively use audiovisual equipment? Was the individual able to work in a lot of facts while keeping the presentation lively and interesting? Did the person use an emotional appeal that persuaded people to accept his or her point of view?

6. Evaluate the relevance of what is being said. Are there any new or useful data being communicated that can be of personal value?

7. Listen for intended meanings as well as for expressed ideas. Is the speaker trying to convey any hidden messages? What are they? How do they influence the overall content of the message?

8. Integrate everything the speaker is saying so that it all fits into a logical composite. If any information does not fit into this overall scheme, put it aside and try to integrate it later.

9. Be a responsive listener. Maintain eye contact with speakers and give them positive feedback, such as nods of agreement and bright facial expressions.

10. Accept the challenge of effective listening. Effective RMs recognize that it is important to communication. In most cases, they have taught themselves to do it well—it is not something with which the RM is born.

The Importance of Speaking and Writing Skills

In recent years, we hear more and more that managers, especially younger managers recently out of our educational system, are unable to speak or write well. As managers move up the hierarchy, these basic communication skills increase in importance. The literature suggests the following guidelines in developing these skills and many effective RMs use them:

1. Know your audience. Before speaking or writing to anyone, effective RMs have an idea of what their audience is interested in hearing or learning about, and gear their message to the audience's interests.
2. Have an attention-getting opener. Make the audience want to learn more. If it is a written communiqué, start with a fact or statistic that the reader may be unaware of and use this to lead into the rest of the message. If it is a formal talk, decide whether a short story or joke is in order. (An after-dinner talk should have one; an in-house presentation to senior level managers should not.) Then briefly relate what the talk is going to be about and begin.
3. Get preliminary feedback on the message. If RMs are giving a talk, they often have a colleague listen and offer suggestions on how they can improve their style. If writing a communiqué, they may have it read over and critiqued by a trusted colleague. RMs use this feedback to improve their overall communication style.
4. Close on a strong point. If giving a talk, effective RMs usually have a story or point for summarizing key points. If it is a report or an extensive memo, this can be done in the last paragraph. If an executive summary of the material is required, they typically put this last paragraph at the front of the paper. An abstract may also be used.

A FINAL WORD

As noted in the earlier empirically based chapters, as well as at the beginning of this chapter, routine communication is a major activity of RMs. In particular, it makes a major contribution to managerial effectiveness. In fact, of the four major activities of RMs uncovered in our research—networking, traditional management functions, human resource management, and routine communication—the communication activity was found to play a more significant role than any of the others for *effective* managers. By contrast, this communication activity did not play as important a role for *successful* RMs. Thus, this chapter on communication primarily concentrated on what effective RMs do. The effective RMs in our study generally do the things suggested in the literature on effective communication; there is a great deal we can learn from them.

7 NETWORKING ACTIVITIES

THE EMPIRICAL BACKDROP

Real managers do networking activities about as frequently as the other major activities. However, our analyses of successful managers (see Chapter 3) showed networking to be by far the most dominant activity. All three analyses techniques (statistical, comparative, and relative strength of relationship) found networking more closely associated to successful RMs than any other activity. Figure 7–1 shows that it had by far the biggest relative contribution to successful RMs. In the effectiveness analysis (see Chapter 4), on the other hand, networking had the least relative impact of any activity. In other words, our study of RMs revealed that networking is definitely related to getting ahead and being successful, but it is not related to being effective. This is perhaps the most consistent finding in our entire study of RMs.

In our investigation of RMs, the *networking activity* was defined as the observable behavioral categories of *socializing/politicking* (nonwork-related chit chat, informal "joking around," discussing rumors, complaining, griping, downgrading others, and gamesmanship) and *interacting with outsiders* (customers, suppliers, vendors, public relations, external meetings, and community service). A more conceptual, comprehensive definition would state that networking is a system of interconnected

Figure 7-1.   Distribution of Networking Activities.

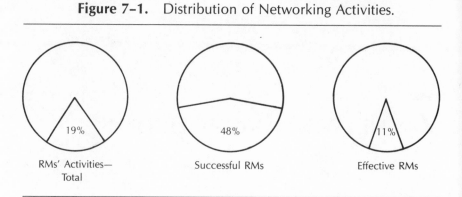

| RMs' Activities— | Successful RMs | Effective RMs |
| Total | | |

or cooperating individuals. It is closely associated with the dynamics of power and the use of social and political skills. One manager explained:

> I have found that the best way to get ahead around here is to be friendly with people. Treat them as individuals. Get to know them; what their backgrounds and interests are. Kid around with them. Then when you need them, they will be there for you, whether it is helping you meet a deadline or giving positive feedback about you when appraisals or promotion time rolls around. I have found that this works with my boss as well as with my subordinates.

This comment describes how RMs network. They use social and political skills to get ahead in their organizations. In this case, the manager is deliberately recognizing and employing networking as a managerial strategy for career success. However, many successful RMs use networking without employing it as a deliberate strategy. But whether a deliberate strategy or not, the results of our study are very clear: the successful RMs exhibit significantly more networking activity (by far more than any other single activity) than do the less successful ones. Equally important, effective RMs (as perceived by subordinate satisfaction, commitment, and organizational effectiveness) do the least amount of this activity.

This chapter explores the various facets of this important, but traditionally overlooked, managerial activity. In particular, networking is examined in light of the informal organization, the dynamics of power, and social/political skills. The chapter then examines the more formal dimensions of networking—mentoring, the usefulness of networks, and the impact of networks.

THE INFORMAL ORGANIZATION—
THE REAL ORGANIZATION

Traditional notions about management and organizations presume that all lines of authority and communication are clearly delineated in the organization chart and policies. This may be true of the *formal* organization (the organization as officially represented by the chart and policies), based on its officially prescribed goals and relationships. These may include official policies representing areas such as equal employee opportunity; advancement of employees on the basis of merit; service to the consumer, client, or patient; product or service quality; and the public good. The chain of command and protocols (who may communicate with whom, with regard to what, how, and when) are usually a matter of written record in the form of company policies and procedures or the organization chart.

Importantly, however, within every formal organization are one or more informal organizations (shadow organizations, if you wish) with unofficial goals, norms, and relationships. These are groups of employees with common beliefs and goals that transcend the formal organization goals. The purpose of this informal organization may be economic, security, or social. The informal groups may be found at the operating level of an organization or in supervisory, staff, or executive levels. Examples include a work-restricting group of production workers or a "good old boy" network of higher level managers who all have relationships quite different than those defined by the formal organization.

Informal organizations, of course, may conflict with the formal organization having competing objectives, restricting output, blocking ambition, or resisting change. But more importantly, the informal organization can also be beneficial to the formal organization. Here are some of the more important functions that informal organizations can have:

- Adding a back-up for the formal organization and providing substantive resources to accomplish formal goals;
- Adding useful supplementary communication channels, especially upward and horizontally;
- Complementing employees' strengths and weaknesses at all levels;
- Reducing the overload on individual employees or groups;

- Motivating employees to reach formally designated goals;
- Satisfying individual and group needs.

In real organizations, informal organizations are inevitable and often very powerful. New RMs are "socialized" into the organization and quickly learn that to survive and succeed, they must also join one or more informal organizations. From the RM's perspective, there is more than one organization to master: the "real" organization is a composite of the formal and informal organizations.

Here are some of the key points to recognize about informal organizations:

- They exist at all levels in every organization.
- They are inevitable.
- They can be beneficial, detrimental, or both, depending on the situation.
- They can be very powerful, even more powerful than the formal organization.
- The "real" organization includes the formal and one or more informal organizations.

POWER: THE NAME OF THE GAME

Besides the informal organization, another inherent dimension of networking is power, which can be defined as the possession of authority, influence, or deliberate control over others. It is inconceivable that RMs can succeed or even survive in modern organizations without power. However, this is an oversimplification because power can also be viewed as a commodity, a medium, or an object of exchange.

Power as a Commodity

It is power as a commodity that is of major concern to successful RMs. Under this interpretation, power is specific. Examples include the ability to affect a specific budget line item, the power to get specific resources to meet a production or report deadline, or the ability to make an impressive "quick showing" (to demonstrate almost immediate results). One manager said:

I have always had the knack of being able to marshall the necessary resources when I really need them, to get the job done. It may be that I ask for a favor from someone or that I demand something from someone else. But if I need something, I get it.

Usually, the discussion of power in the popular management literature is oversimplified. Technically, there are several classifications of power, dealing with the sources of power, the situations under which power is to be used, and the value systems of the persons to be influenced by power (targets of influence).

To begin with, power, unlike love, does not grow with sharing. It cannot be *simultaneously* shared, because inevitably one sharer can, or must, preempt the power of another. Therefore, power can be depicted as a zero-sum-gain model: if one person gains power, the other loses. However, this does not mean that all power relationships are win-lose situations. The key word here is "simultaneously." Power can be shared when it does not compete for the same resource at the same time. Many less successful RMs were unaware of this principle of the power game and consequently: they sought to obtain all of the power all of the time (absolute power), which maximizes conflict; or they assumed that existing power relationships were unchangeable—they either gave up or they attempted to get things done with insufficient power (thereby limiting their success).

Collectively, all of the available power (defined here as the control of resources) can be found in the formal and informal organizations. The successful RM, like the one cited earlier, literally must acquire control of resources either on a formal demand or an informal "favor" basis to use power effectively. The ability to obtain such control, without alienating informal colleagues or formal superiors, is a significant "litmus test" that distinguishes successful RMs from their less successful counterparts. Empirically, this conclusion was verified in our study by the finding that the successful RMs engaged in relatively more observed gamesmanship and, especially among higher level RMs, managing conflict (for example, appealing to higher authority or third-party negotiators).

The Use of Power: Maintaining a Balance

More successful RMs are not only using power, but are able to maintain a delicate balance between impotence and empire-building. They are also selective about the amounts and kinds of power to acquire; thus, their leadership style is critical to their success. This observation of RM success is consistent with three currently popular theoretical propositions in the literature about characteristics supposedly common to successful managers.

First is the notion of "cognitive complexity": successful managers may have more complicated thinking processes than nonsuccessful managers. It follows from this theoretical proposition that successful managers are more capable of dealing with the increasing complexity found in today's organizations. Closely related is the only conclusive result that has come out of the trait theories of leadership—that leaders are more intelligent than their average followers. Successful managers are able to consider an array of facts and exploding information in order to develop effective strategies and tactics to obtain the power to make good decisions and get them implemented. This takes "raw" intelligence. One successful manager commented:

> The main reason I feel I have been relatively successful around here is that I can do the simple things like read faster and remember better than my colleagues. For example, I sit on the finance committee. I have no trouble understanding or remembering the data that is constantly being thrown at us. Brad, on the other hand, just can't get it through his head. The boss, of course, notices this also, and while I am getting excellent appraisals and am due for a promotion, Brad is in trouble.

Third is the notion that most, if not all, successful managers share a strong need for power. This need is expressed as the need to be in charge, the need to manipulate others. Most people view such needs in negative terms. Harvard psychologist David McClelland, however, describes this need for power in two dimensions, or "faces." The negative face he calls "personal power," which is the power characterized by manipulation and personal gain at the expense of others. In contrast, he also proposes another face of power, which he calls "social power." This type of power need is concerned with helping the group to get ahead and is characterized by a group identity, as in "*our* department is going to be the best in the company," not "*I* am going to really look good so *I* can get promoted," as in the drive for personal power.

In other words, social power needs are more concerned with the kinds of goals managers set, and their effect on the self-esteem and growth of subordinates. McClelland has evidence that the social-power motivated managers may be more effective than personal-power types.

Importantly, however, those with intense personal power needs may be successful, especially if they keep mobile. One subordinate of a personal-power-oriented manager commented:

> He has been successful all right. He has always kept one step ahead of the wolves. The decisions he makes in our department make him look good in the eyes of upper management. But those of us who have to carry out his decisions know that they are really not the best for the goals of the company as a whole. I suppose it will only be a matter of time before he gets another big promotion and we will be left holding his bag of problems.

Thus, personal power needs may lead to success in getting ahead in the organization, but not necessarily effectiveness. This, of course, may help explain why we found such a contrast between the high use of networking by successful RMs and its minimal use by effective RMs in our studies. Yet, personal power may be a prerequisite to the maintenance and exercise of social power. In other words, as in the other dimensions of RMs, there is probably no "best" type of power. Each may be necessary, depending on the situation.

In summary, here are some key points to remember about power:

- Successful RMs need power.
- The same power can be time-shared, but not simultaneously shared.
- The process of acquiring power can be complicated but seems crucial to RMs' success.
- There are several kinds of power.
- Although personal power needs seem to be more related to success, they do not seem to be related to effectiveness.

SOCIAL SKILLS FOR SUCCESS

We found social skills to be a more important ingredient in networking than even the dynamics of the informal organization and power. Social skills are closely related to the socialization process and group dynamics. However, social skills also include an understanding and sensitivity of RMs to their own self-management and perspectives.

New managers usually work hard to develop such social skills. It is important to success to recognize that these social skills are not permanent, and as with all skills, they can deteriorate with disuse. For example, managers in dead-end jobs, doing the same kind of work over a long period of time, seem to develop jaded perspectives of their own social skills.

This was demonstrated by one of the RMs in our study who was approaching retirement age. He was a hard worker all his life and, as many RMs do, translated his personal experience and beliefs about work into something like a religion. His beliefs were so firm and structured that he regarded those who had differing work-related views with contempt. Although this manager had reached a fairly high level because of his long seniority in an organization of more than 300 employees, he was not really successful in terms of our definition of success (level, tenure) used in the study. Looking deeper into his career path, we found that undoubtedly because of his drive and capacity for hard work, he had been a very successful middle manager early on. Now, operating from experience, he grew intolerant of those with less drive and experience. When his subordinates or peers disagreed with him, or when they made constructive suggestions, he often responded with anger and abusive language. Consequently, although he was entrenched (and could not realistically be fired), he became an organizational pariah. The director of personnel was concerned that, having experienced one heart attack, this RM might not survive a second—and that he was making his work life stressful enough to induce a second attack.

This RM himself revealed to us that he had a similar perspective. He had substantial income-producing property and didn't really need the job. But he regarded compromise as a threat to the power he had worked hard to attain. He felt alienated and isolated—"surrounded by enemies" who were "out to get him." He really wanted to retire to lead a more relaxed life on his farm. Obviously, he needed professional help, but he refused. Finally, the personnel manager ordered him to get the help he needed, on medical grounds. Failure to comply would forfeit his retirement and survivor benefits. Several months later, he retired voluntarily.

This example illustrates the close relationship between social skills and support networks. This RM lacked any social skills at this point in his career and operated within a rigid structure of his own creation. His dogmatic approach to work, and life in general, denied any reciprocal social influence. As a result, he had no support network when he needed it as a manager, or for his very survival. He was no longer able to compromise; he had backed himself into an almost inescapable corner. From his perspective, he couldn't accept the fact that he lacked sufficient social skills to get along with anyone (up, down, or horizontally). As long as he believed that his retirement benefits would accrue to his survivors, he didn't even care if he died as a result of the conflict and stress he had helped to create. The personnel director, on the other hand, was more socially skillful. She used and enlarged her social skills in trying to solve this difficult personnel problem to benefit herself, the organization, and the ailing manager.

POLITICAL SKILLS FOR SUCCESS

Closely related are political skills. Politics, like power, often have negative connotations. As used here "politics" and "political skills" refer to the practice of guiding and influencing organizational outcomes to one's own ends. They do not refer to artful or dishonest influence of those outcomes.

There are many political skills that can be employed by successful RMs. Which political strategy is used depends on the information and resources available to managers from their networking connections. Here is a sampling of some commonly used political strategies found in the literature that would be supported by successful RMs in conjunction with their networking activities:

1. *Divide and rule.* Those who are divided may choose to form their own networks.
2. *Maintain alliances with powerful people.* This includes networking with members of important departments, strategically placed secretaries, staff assistants, or anyone close to powerful people.
3. *Embrace or demolish.* When a new manager takes over an organization, high-level managers should be either warmly welcomed or terminated. If they are downgraded and retained, they will remain determined to recover their lost power. If so, the information afforded through networking is essential for the new manager to be effective.
4. *Collect and use IOUs.* This strategy is an integral part of networking. Failing to pay IOUs when called due adversely affects both membership in networks and the attainment of power in the organization. Here, more than in any other aspect of managerial success, there is no "free lunch."
5. *Manipulate scarce information.* If information is to be used as a commodity to gain power, networks can expand the sources of such information.
6. *Make a quick showing.* To look good on a task right away may require supplementary resources. These may be available only through networking.

7. *Wait for a crisis.* Opportunities to develop and use political skills
    are often present when the organization is in trouble. Programmed
    decisionmaking is relaxed and opportunities for brilliant success
    or ignominious failure are greatly increased.
8. *Avoid decisive engagement.* To use an evolutionary, rather than
    a revolutionary, approach and to avoid "ruffling feathers" requires
    reliable knowledge of the pitfalls to avoid. This kind of informa-
    tion, almost never available through the formal organization, is
    often available only through networking channels.
9. *Progress gradually.* Seek a foothold through small changes, then
    use this as a basis for larger accomplishments. Networking can
    provide the information to get this done discreetly.

In one organization, when a male employee was promoted over two
qualified female employees, the women decided to use political skills
to address the issue. The women organized an after-work discussion
group, inviting outsiders to talk about women's careers. Although
discussion formally focused on relatively bland subjects, the political
strategy of these meetings was to develop a shared belief that the career
development of women in this company was arrested by a congenial,
but chauvinist, personnel manager. They were convinced that a formal confrontation would have produced much conflict, but little change.
Instead, these women deliberately set out to change the manager's
behavior systematically, slowly teasing him at first. In time, he recognized that he had been targeted and labeled. As a result, he really had
no graceful alternative but to confer the next promotion to a woman.
There are several important points that come out of this example.
First, an informal group recognized a common problem and formed
a network to solve it. This network developed a strategy. Second, the
network provided the group members with influence (power) that was
otherwise unavailable to them as isolated individuals. And third,
through political skills of the network members, the problem was
solved. Importantly, this process worked beneficially in both directions—to the female organizational members and to the male manager.

MENTORING: A SPECIFIC NETWORKING STRATEGY

A specific networking strategy that many women RMs and others have
used successfully to get ahead is mentoring. The mentor is usually a

powerful manager who sponsors a protégé. In the process, the subordinate (the protégé) acquires a teacher, psychological and social support, confidence, assistance, access to resources, a degree of protection, and an advocate. Mentors, simultaneously, acquire help in doing their jobs, new information, loyal followers and associates, prestige given by the protégés, expansion of their power base, and a reputation as starmakers. In other words, this mentoring process is a win-win networking strategy for both the mentor and the protégé.

However, as in all networking, there are also certain risks and costs involved. Mentoring takes time—time to develop a network of obligations owed to you and time to reciprocate favors. Another problem is that the protégé may fail, reflecting discredit on the mentor. There is always the risk of bringing an incompetent into the network. Just as the prestige of each is shared, the infamy of each is also shared. The mentor risks choosing an incompetent protégé or one who develops into a corporate leper. Similarly, should the mentor for some reason become a corporate pariah, the protégé risks being tarred with the same brush.

THE USEFULNESS OF FORMAL NETWORKS TO RMs

The socializing and politicking (that is, networking) behaviors observed among our successful RMs are in some ways consistent with the traditional notion of success-oriented managers. In theory, and in our empirical evidence, many success-driven managers try to develop useful networks (with others both inside and outside their work settings). Why then are some RMs more successful than others? Is it a matter of luck, or is something else involved? Even members of formal networks seem to experience varying degrees of career success. Let's take a look at some formal networks and the kinds of success experienced by their members.

There are many examples of networks within formal organizations. One formal network, which became a company-sanctioned group and grew tenfold during a ten-year period, has no legitimate (official) power in the formal organization. Its power is found instead in the informal network. This informal network shapes employee attitudes and affects company policies. In fact, these informal networks shape the organizational culture. Consequently, members of the network share more power in the organization than do nonmembers. This suggests a form of "unionism," which is *not* the purpose of networking. Successful RMs may rely too heavily on the power of membership in the network per se, rather than on the productive use of the network to get the job done and accomplish performance goals.

Networks offer powerful influences for their members. Some formal networks have scheduled meetings, are visited by corporate officers who provide useful information, and conduct activities targeted to individual career development. Formal networks, proliferating widely, can offer information that affects assignments, promotion, and basic career matters.

With all the publicity given formal networks, and with the stereotype of the old boy network, it isn't surprising that some RMs are misled into believing that membership is all that is required. It's easy to overlook the "exchange ratio," the proportion of inputs versus outcomes for the real manager. Membership in a network is no insurance against exploitation of either the member or the network. Just as many of us have difficulty translating theory into practice, membership in a network—either formal or informal—is of little value if it cannot be translated into performance.

THE IMPACT OF NETWORKS

Networks can provide RMs at all levels with information vital to their success. Networks can help RMs answer important questions such as the following:

- Who has the final word on approvals?
- Who has the final word documenting a change?
- Who does one approach for restricted or confidential information?
- What strategies are most effective to get the job done in a visible way?
- How does one sell top-level management on proposed ideas or changes?
- Who controls the release of financial records for review?
- How does one obtain referrals to and from other network members?
- How and by whom is two-way feedback channeled?

In other words, networks help RMs in the socialization process. We conclusively found in our study that networks enhance RMs' organizational success, as defined by the promotion index.

Our study results indicated that although definitely related to career success of RMs, networking may not be related to their effectiveness.

Despite its many functional attributes for success, networking may also be dysfunctional if the RM uses it in inappropriate situations. For instance, networking provides managers with friendly support that can be called upon in time of need or for getting ahead, but it does not excuse managers from doing their homework (for example, being prepared for a budget meeting). The effectiveness of networking may depend a great deal on credibility. Factors affecting managerial effectiveness of networking may be similar to factors affecting organizational effectiveness in general. Included would be factors such as the following:

- The amount of reciprocal trust among members;
- The degree of interdependence among members and how this is orchestrated;
- Common goals among participants; and
- Credibility and quality of resources.

Here are some possible guidelines that can be used to make networking more effective:

- Ask questions—don't make assumptions.
- Don't be boring—listen.
- Return favors promptly, in measure of quantity and quality.
- Don't lose contacts—follow up, keep in touch, report back.
- Be businesslike and professional in the network; satisfy personal and social needs elsewhere.
- Ask for what you need.
- Help others, be useful, follow through.
- Be discreet—don't tell everything to everybody.
- Know your own limitations; don't expect miracles from others in the network.
- Conduct post mortems on your networking failures for clues to succeed in future attempts.

It is becoming increasingly clear that networking may be able to influence both the hiring and turnover processes of today's organizations. The influence of networking on hiring through "connections" has always been recognized; more recent research has found that networking can affect employee turnover. Networking tends to be quite positive with regard to retaining employees. For example, studies find a lower turnover rate among employees who knew people in the organization prior to employment than among those who knew no one prior to being hired. This finding is usually explained by the more realistic job previews and additional information that these new employees may have about their organizations. Other studies find that persons in authority are connected to more network channels than are persons with little or no authority. This finding supports our studies' conclusions that successful RMs do more networking activity, acquire control of resources (power), and thus, are more likely to be sought after as "connections."

There is also evidence that the specific organizational situation helps determine and control the freedom of participants to change from one network to another. This is based on the proposition that social homogeneity (everyone thinks and behaves alike) reduces uncertainty in the organization. This is probably true with regard to internal work activities but may not hold up in the broader social context (that is, social networks cross organizational lines). It is virtually impossible to keep networks purely social or purely work-related. Even those networks that are formally designated and supposedly professional in nature have inviolate social rules. Much evidence, including our own studies, suggests that the long-term influence of networking is a reciprocal, interactive process between each member and its related organizational and social context. This dynamic process profoundly affects outcomes such as promotions and career success.

WHAT WE CAN LEARN FROM REAL MANAGERS

There are a number of important lessons that can be learned from real managers concerning the often overlooked managerial activity of networking. These lessons, derived from our study of RMs, can be briefly summarized as follows:

1. Successful RMs do relatively more networking activity than their less successful counterparts.
2. Networking is the least strongly related activity to RM effectiveness.
3. Networking seems indispensable to RMs seeking to acquire and retain power.
4. Networking can tap unique social and political skills of RMs.
5. Besides the informal networks that emerge in organizational dynamics, formally created networks, such as women's networks or

mentoring, can be beneficial to their members and can help accomplish goals of certain groups as well as individuals.

6. Although there are no guarantees for success or causal relationships from networking, the risk of failure without networking is clearly higher than it is with networking.

8 HUMAN RESOURCES MANAGEMENT ACTIVITIES

THE EMPIRICAL BACKDROP

Although the human resource management activities have the same relative frequency of occurrence as do the other activities, they make the *least* contribution to successful real managers but, after communication, the *greatest* contribution to effective real managers. In the success analysis, human resources management activities were last in the relative strength of relationship analysis; the comparative analysis found that the top third of successful RMs did about 25 percent less of these activities than did the bottom third. In the effectiveness analysis, however, these activities came in a strong second in terms of relative strength of relationship. As Figure 8-1 illustrates, RMs are doing human resource management activities, but the successful ones are *not* giving as much relative attention to them. Importantly, however, there seems to be a strong relationship between these activities and RMs effectiveness.

Human resource management, by its very nature, and as defined in our study, is much more multidimensional than the other activities. The following behavioral categories constituted the *human resource management* activities in our study: *motivating/reinforcing, managing conflict, disciplining/punishing, staffing,* and *training/developing.* Table 8-1 provides some actual examples drawn from the interviews. The following

Figure 8–1.   Distribution of Human Resources Management
Activities.

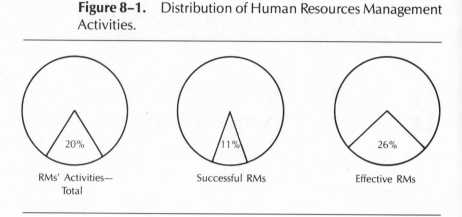

20%	11%	26%
RMs' Activities— Total	Successful RMs	Effective RMs

sections examine these activities in greater depth and discuss, using examples from our qualitative data and interaction with RMs, the human resources management implications.

MOTIVATING AND REINFORCING

Motivation is a complex psychological process, but can be defined simply as a desire or need that drives someone toward a goal or incentive. For certain needs, such as achievement or self-esteem, the goal or the reward may be money, promotion, or recognition. In any event, regardless of the motivational cause, from a behavioral (or more technically an operant) perspective, behavior is a function of its consequences. If the behavior has a reinforcing consequence, the subsequent behavioral frequency will increase. If behavior has a punishing consequence, the subsequent behavior will decrease.

Joining motivation and reinforcement as a human resource management activity follows managers' activities as they try to understand their people's needs, fulfill these needs, and then reinforce those behaviors that contribute to performance goals. The observable behaviors representing the activity of *motivating and reinforcing* included things such as increasing job challenge, listening to suggestions, conveying appreciation and recognition, providing performance feedback, and allocating formal rewards (see Table 2–1). The following sections examine each of these in turn and provide representative accounts of how real managers actually carry out these motivating/reinforcing behaviors in their human resource management activities.

Increasing Job Challenge

There are a number of ways RMs increase job challenge. One is by increasing the amount of autonomy. The literature suggests and effective RMs would verify that people tend to be motivated by jobs that offer them freedom, independence, and discretion in scheduling the work and determining how to carry it out. One manager commented:

> My people don't need me looking over their shoulders every five minutes. What I do is tell them what needs to be done and when it should be accomplished. I don't care how fast they work just as long as work is done on time. If they want to take twenty minutes for coffee rather than the usual ten minutes, that's fine with me. They can even go to lunch a little early. And if I see them in the corridor or in one another's office talking, I don't care. It's up to them how they get the work done. My job is seeing that it's done on time and done right. Aside from this, I try to stay out of their way and not overcontrol the job.

Effective RMs also increase job challenge by giving their people authority to control their own work. For example, if Group A is responsible for producing computer disk drives and Group B's job is to test these drives to see that they have been built correctly, there is an inevitable conflict. Group B is controlling Group A to the extent that Group B either passes or rejects Group A's work. To overcome this potential problem, some RMs have given their work groups the equipment and authority to check their own work. In this way, the group becomes accountable for its own work, and if there is a problem, the group can then rework the unit and fix it. In addition, effective RMs reinforce the individual and the group with contingent feedback and recognition for taking on the added responsibility and correcting quality problems.

Another effective approach is to make people realize the significance of their work. Quite often, RMs have found that when their people are aware of the important role they play, their motivation potential increases. One manager used this tactic:

> We often have customers come to the plant to see how we build these units. Sometimes it's new customers, but quite often they have been buying from us for the last couple of years and we've invited them in as a public relations gesture. During these visits I like to get some of the customers off to the side to visit with some of my people down on the line. I have the customer explain to them how important their work is from a safety standpoint. If one of these units is built wrong, a major accident could take place. Once my people realize how much others are depending on them to build the unit right, their motivation to produce a "no defects" product seems to go up.

Table 8-1.   Human Resource Management Activities:
Some Specific Examples Drawn from Structured
Interviews.

Motivating/Reinforcing Personnel		
High Amount	Medium Amount	Low Amount
Writes a letter about what a fine job the individual did and puts a copy into the person's personnel file.	Calls the individual into the office and verbally praises the person for a job well done.	Tells the person in passing, "You did a good job."

Disciplining/Punishing		
High Amount	Medium Amount	Low Amount
Fires an individual for continually being late.	Writes a formal reprimand on a worker who is continually late and puts it in the individual's personnel file.	Yells at a worker for continually being late.

Managing Conflict		
High Amount	Medium Amount	Low Amount
Calls involved workers together and discusses the situations with them in an effort to arrive at a solution acceptable to all.	Makes a decision regarding how to resolve the conflict and tells those involved what it is.	Separates those who are involved so that arguments and personal interaction are minimized.

Staffing		
High Amount	Medium Amount	Low Amount
Reviews all personnel records and conducts interviews among those who have applied for the job; then makes a decision.	Sets hiring criteria, reduces the list of candidates based on these criteria, and then makes a decision regarding whom to hire.	Uses hiring criteria to determine who is the best and makes a decision as quickly as possible given this information.

Table 8-1.   *(continued)*

High Amount	Training/Developing Medium Amount	Low Amount
Identifies training and development needs throughout the department or unit and then coordinates with the people who are responsible for providing this training.	Personally determines the types of training and development that unit personnel need and sends this information to those who are responsible for providing this training.	Has personnel identify the types of training and development they feel they need and encourages them to attend seminars and programs that will provide it.

Listening to Suggestions

Another approach to motivating/reinforcing used by effective RMs is to listen to suggestions. Quite often when there is a problem or something needs to be done differently, the operating employee knows the best approach to use or the one solution that will work. One manager told us this story:

> We had a problem meeting our department's standards. No matter how hard we tried, we always seemed to fall 10 to 15 percent short of the recognized standard. I called a meeting and asked everyone for suggestions about what we could do. A couple of the people pointed out that the time allocated for assembling the units was way too short. In particular, one of the parts was supposed to be installed in fifty-five seconds but the fastest time they could get it done in was eighty-five seconds. The general manager sent down a design engineer and he checked the part against the blueprints. It was built exactly as called for in the specs. However, when we asked him to assemble it, it took the engineer over two minutes. The problem was that the part was too big and it had to be worked into the unit, rather than adjusted and then snapped in. The engineer redesigned the blueprint and ever since we've been able to meet the standard.

A closely related approach is active listening. Active listening involves letting the other person talk without giving any direction or advice. Any responses from the manager should be used to seek clarification or extension of the explanation, rather than offering guidance or support. Typical responses from actively listening RMs include, "You seem quite upset over this matter," "I see," and "What else?" In each case, the objective is to keep the other person talking. Quite often, this approach is cathartic. It is particularly useful in motivating/reinforcing subordinates who are upset over some event and want their boss to know about it. A representative example comes from a manager whose company had announced an end to overtime:

> When Greg came in here, he was really mad. He felt his people relied heavily on overtime to supplement their base pay and he felt that management's decision was going to wreak havoc on his people. I just let him talk. He had a right to be angry. Top management had often pointed out that because of overtime we were able to pay higher annual take-home pay than anyone else in the local area. They really were pushing overtime as a part of the total compensation package. When management suddenly cut it out because of a supposed downturn in sales, we were all shocked. When Greg finished, we just sat here and looked at each other for a couple of minutes. Then he got up and said, "Thanks for listening," went back to his office, and that was it. I later heard he called his people together, backed management to the hilt, and told them that the company had been good to them over the years and they should be thankful that overtime had lasted this long. His unit is still one of the best we've got.

Conveying Appreciation and Recognition

There are a number of ways of reinforcing people. One is simply to convey appreciation and recognition to them. This can be done in two ways: verbal and written. Verbal appreciation and recognition occur on a face-to-face basis. "You did a nice job on the industrial products account," "I saw your monthly sales projections and you're doing great work," and "Nice going. That last monthly report you submitted was excellent," are all examples. Verbal communication is more widely used than written because it is easier to provide and it can be used in reinforcing any type of performance from lackluster but improving ("You're really getting a lot better.") to outstanding ("Your sales are the highest we ever had in a three-month period!"). Many effective RMs use reinforcement on a day-to-day basis to foster motivation, often using their own version of management by walking around. One effective manager used this technique:

> Every day I make it a point to look at performance data from the day before. In this way I know how well each of my people is doing. This is important

if I'm going to get out there and reinforce them on a daily basis. Once I've reviewed the data, I begin making my daily rounds. Those who have done a good job hear about it from me. Those who haven't are offered encouragement—unless their performance has been down for three to four days. Then I make it a point to call them over to the side and talk with them and offer my help to get them back on track. You know what? My people like the fact that I know how well they're doing. They know I wouldn't pay attention if I didn't care.

Written praise and recognition is particularly important when someone has done something that merits formal recognition. Many effective RMs use it as documentation for the individual's personnel file. For example, in one case a RM reported that three of her people had developed a new major cost-saving suggestion. The company gave each of these individuals a financial reward for the suggestion. However, the RM went further and sent each a personal memo relating how important their suggestion had been and praising them for it. A copy of the memo was put into each of their personnel files.

Performance Feedback

One of the most powerful ways that effective RMs can reinforce/motivate their people is by providing them with performance feedback. The characteristics of effective performance feedback available to all RMs can perhaps best be summarized by the acronym PIGS—positive, immediate, graphic, and specific. Table 8–2 depicts such PIGS feedback. First, feedback should be positive. People do not like to listen to negative feedback. Even if bad news is being conveyed, it should be done in a positive way. Second, the feedback should be immediate or be given as soon as possible. Third, if possible, the feedback should be presented graphically rather than in columns of numerical data. A graph does a lot more to provide feedback than does a computer printout. People can "see" a graph a lot easier than a printout. Finally, the feedback should be as specific as possible. If it can be quantified, it should be. One manager used this feedback method:

> The accounting people provide us with these neatly bound figures every quarter. Frankly, I have trouble figuring them out myself, let alone passing this data on down to my people, so the reports just accumulate over in the corner there. Lately, though, I have been posting our weekly production figures on a graph. I personally keep it up to date, on the wall of our employee lounge. I see them gather around this graph all the time and they seem to

Table 8-2.   "PIGS" Feedback.

<u>P</u>OSITIVE	Feedback has to be positive. People will not listen to negative feedback. There is a positive and negative side to everything; talk about uptime rather than downtime, attendance rather than absenteeism.
<u>I</u>MMEDIATE	"Real time" feedback is the best—the sooner the better. Quarterly reports and annual performance appraisals are not sufficient. Ideally, feedback should happen simultaneously with the performance behavior itself, as in some jobs and in self-feedback systems. If not simultaneously, then the feedback should be given hourly, daily, or in some cases, weekly, but not longer.
<u>G</u>RAPHIC	Feedback should be visual. Computer printout sheets are not sufficient. Put the feedback data into a graph whenever possible. This gives the employee an instant look at the past, present, and future trends. A single graph is worth a hundred pages of computer printout.
<u>S</u>PECIFIC	The feedback should be as specific as possible. It should be quantified as much as possible and be stated in relation to a goal. It should be job and performance related, not personally related.

know where we stand. The productivity rate has definitely gone up since I started doing this. I can show you the graph to prove it to you.

Allocating Formal Rewards

The allocation of formal rewards is the most obvious way of motivating/ reinforcing human resources. There are two basic formal rewards available in today's organizations: pay and promotion.

Wage and salary increases take two primary forms: across-the-board and merit. Across-the-board pay increases are given to everyone and have limited reinforcing/motivating value, because they do not consider performance. A good example is 5 percent for all middle managers and supervisors and 4 percent for all hourly people. Merit pay, on the other hand, involves RM judgment and appraisal in allocating discretionary funds contingent upon performance. An example is 8 percent for the best employees, 4 percent for average employees, and nothing for everyone else. Unfortunately, most organizations make heaviest use of across-the-board increases, especially in times of limited pay raises.

Many RMs expressed little support of merit pay because it often involves giving a lot of money to a small percentage of employees and very little to the rest. Most organizations today have adopted a combination approach, allocating most of the money for across-the-board raises and a small percentage for merit.

The biggest problem with this mixed approach is that high performers tend to receive very little extra for their efforts. Thus motivation to maintain this level of output is often reduced or has to be made up through the nature of the work, that is, making the work interesting and challenging. On the other hand, to the extent that the RM can tie pay to performance, the pay will be a reinforcer/motivator.

In many cases, an organization can sidestep the across-the-board/ merit pay dilemma by simply promoting deserving individuals and giving them the higher pay that goes along with the new position. To the extent that people desire promotion, this is an effective motivation/reinforcement strategy. However, it must be closely aligned with the training and development dimension of human resource management (discussed later in the chapter) to ensure that the individual is not pushed ahead too fast. Effective RMs recognize that some individuals do not want to be promoted and doing so results in problems for both the person and the organization, as this example shows:

> Every year I recommend my two best people for promotions. Since we promote from within, both are usually moved up within a three-to-six month time period. There's a lot of upward mobility around here because we have been expanding so quickly. However, I always make it a point to talk to my people before recommending them for anything. I learned this lesson the hard way. A few years back I strongly recommended a person who turned out to be a real dud. Not even extra training and development could help him. Why? Because he simply didn't want to be a manager. He liked working where he was and felt threatened by the increased responsibility. I made the mistake of thinking that a promotion is an important motivator without considering the individual's personal desires. For some people, doing things they're good at is more important than moving on to increased responsibilities and managing others.

DISCIPLINING AND PUNISHING

Although disciplining/punishing was observed so infrequently in our study that it was dropped from our analysis of successful and effective

RMs, it nevertheless is an important dimension of human resource management activities. Just as it is questionable that motivation and reinforcement can (or technically should) be categorized together, it should also be recognized that there is a difference between discipline and punishment.

Discipline does not always have to be punitive. In fact, discipline is most often used to prevent certain behaviors from occurring in the future while punishment, unfortunately, often becomes an end in itself. Punishment, contingently administered, will decrease the frequency of subsequent behavior. However, the problem with the use of punishment in managing human resources is that it tends to change (or actually suppress) the behavior only temporarily and it tends to generate such undesirable side effects as hate and revenge. Discipline, on the other hand, can be more useful in human resource management because it can be preventative and minimize the side-effect problems of punishment. Two discipline strategies suggested in the literature and supported by effective RMs could be labeled "little by little" and "room for adjustment."

Little-by-Little Strategy

Discipline can take a number of different forms. However, most effective disciplinary processes employ what is called progressive discipline. Under this strategy the effective RM begins with an oral warning. If this corrects the problem, nothing more is done. If not, a second disciplinary step, more severe than the first, is taken. As this pattern continues, the effective RM begins applying more and more sanctions until the employee is given the final disciplinary action, dismissal.

A typical pattern of progressive discipline used by many organizations has four phases: an oral warning; a written warning, which is placed in the individual's personnel file; a disciplinary layoff (this will vary in length from one day to two weeks, depending on the nature of problem); and discharge.

This is only one pattern of discipline. Realistically, especially in unionized firms, RMs may be unable to fire a person without collecting considerable "hard" evidence to back up their charge, and even then, it may be necessary to submit the entire matter to arbitration. Nevertheless, no matter how the progressive discipline process is set up, there are five characteristics that the literature suggests should be present.

These characteristics establish the parameters within which this particular strategy is executed. Each is important to effective RMs in their administration of discipline. They are the following:

1. *Discipline should be immediate.* As soon as the effective RM checks the facts and knows that a rule or policy has been violated, discipline should follow. This immediacy establishes a causal link between the act and the discipline. Waiting to take disciplinary action only weakens this linkage.
2. *There should be advanced warning.* Rules and policies should be made clear to all employees, and they should know what the penalties are for breaking them. If there is an orientation period for new employees, this information should be disseminated and explained at that time.
3. *Rules should be kept to a minimum.* People tend to remember and follow only a few rules. When the number of rules becomes too great, violations increase. Employees simply cannot remember all the rules and, because there are so many of them to follow, they tend to believe that none of them are really important.
4. *Discipline should be consistent.* Individuals who commit the same offense should be given the same discipline. Because everyone has had advanced warning and knows the rules, the penalties should be consistent from one person to the next.
5. *Discipline should be impersonal.* Everyone should be treated equally from the shop steward to the operating employee to the president's secretary. Who they are should not influence the type of disciplinary action taken against them.

Room-for-Adjustment Strategy

Effective RMs find that some form of punitive action is sometimes necessary, but often only as a last resort. The literature suggests there are a number of guidelines and effective RMs tend to follow these. First, RMs clarify *why* the action is being taken, then clearly tie the punishment to the rule violation. The third step gives the people being punished a chance to modify or change their behavior and thus avoid future action. However, there is difficulty in using punishment effectively. One manager commented:

Taking punitive action against one of my people is no fun. I really hate it. But it has to be done from time to time, if only to show the others that proper behavior is expected. Whenever I have to do this, there is one rule I always follow: let the person know what was wrong and how this can be avoided in the future. I never just tell someone that he's done something wrong, lower the boom on him, and walk away. I always come back at the first opportunity and tell the person punished when they did it right. This seems to help and they don't hold a grudge or feel they have to get back at me somehow.

MANAGING CONFLICT

Besides the obvious human resource management behaviors of motivating/reinforcing and disciplining/punishing, our study also found conflict-managing behaviors in this activity of RMs. Particularly in recent times, one of the most common causes of conflict is the lack of resources and the subsequent competition for them. For example, an organization that is working out next year's budget is likely to find that the requests of the major department heads are greater than the total amount available. As a result, some (if not all) of the department heads are going to get less than they requested. Many department heads will jockey for position and campaign to improve their chances for the largest relative share of the budgetary allocations. Data will be compiled to show the positive effect of giving their department its request and the negative effect of cutting this amount. Inevitably, some departments lose, others win. Both during and after this budgetary battle, conflict is a common occurrence.

A second common example of conflict occurs when the organization is unionized and there is an adversary union-management relationship. Each side often tries to discredit the other or prevent it from attaining its objectives. Still another source of conflict in today's organizations is interindividual or intragroup conflict that occurs when superior-subordinate pairs or members of a department group are unable to get along with each other. Quite often the departments or conflicting parties involved undermine one another's efforts. In managing these and other types of conflict, effective RMs rely upon a number of approaches. The following examines three commonly found in the human resource management literature.

Cooperation and Cooptation

Probably the most common way that effective RMs manage conflict is to seek cooperation among the conflicting parties. They try to have the conflicting parties put aside their differences and focus on the overall objective. If they can do this, the conflict can be solved at this point. However, it seldom is this easy. Some action is typically required. Effective RMs often try to find out what the problem is and then restructure the situation so as to reduce or eliminate the problem. One manager took this approach:

> I found that about half the members of the department were upset with the other half. I really don't know how long this infighting had been going on; I guess for a couple of years before I got here. I know that both factions got along fine with their own members, but that there was friction whenever cooperation between them was needed. I reorganized the unit and split it into two completely different parts. Now each group works independently of the other and productivity is higher than it has ever been. I know this isn't necessarily the ideal solution, but it took care of our problem, at least for the time being.

Another way effective RMs manage conflict is cooptation. This involves making the parties in the conflict part of the solution by forcing them to get involved. The strategy is particularly effective when those causing the conflict are interested in doing a good job but feel that the organization or their manager is ignoring them. One manager gave us this example:

> Every month we would get our computer printouts and use them to evaluate progress in the various units. Every month four of the supervisors in our group would complain that the printouts did not provide them with the right kinds of information for controlling operations. I got pretty steamed up after a while and said, "Okay, if you want a different type of printout, you design it. I'm appointing you as a committee of four. Go out to the field, find out what kinds of information we should be getting from those units, and coordinate your efforts with the computer staff to design and implement a system that will do what you think needs to be done." I didn't hear anymore griping for the next two weeks. However, when the group came in with its revised form, I had to admit it was a lot better than what we had been using. They were right with their complaints. Today, we're much better able to monitor our field units than we were a year ago.

Higher Authority

Sometimes conflict is so bad that it cannot be handled first-hand by the manager. Support from higher management is required. This is particularly true when managers are new at their jobs and their subordinates have been around for quite a while. No matter how hard many new RMs try to resolve a conflict, they are ineffective because the experienced subordinates refuse to accept their authority in this situation.

> When I took over I was the first woman manager they ever had around here. Everyone regarded me as nothing more than a token to help our EEO statistics. As a result, when I found that two of my experienced people were squabbling over some petty matter and called them in and told them to start cooperating, I couldn't get anywhere with them. However, this didn't last long. I explained the situation to my boss and he backed me up. He called both of these people into his office and spelled out the rules for them. This not only got me through my authority crisis in the department, but it handled the conflict problems as well. I'll admit that I haven't gone back for help since—but if I need it, I, and my people, know it's there.

Third-Party Negotiators

Sometimes effective RMs use conflict management techniques that fall between the two extremes described above. Someone is brought in from the outside who has no direct authority to make the parties in the conflict do anything. The role of such a third party (it may be a neutral person inside the organization or someone from the outside) is to influence and persuade or simply to negotiate, rather than to order or coerce the conflicting parties. In one case, an effective RM said he had been unable to get sufficient cooperation from two of his operating employees in a union shop. Rather than write them up or take any form of disciplinary action, he alerted the shop steward about what was going on. The steward talked to both people and that was the end of it. Here is an example of bringing in a mutually respected third party:

> I had some people in my department who were upset because we had installed computer equipment without consulting them. They complained that the equipment was too difficult to operate and they didn't understand the programs they were supposed to be using. I'll bet my junior high school child could have understood that material. These people just didn't want to learn how to use the machine. I handled the situation in two simple steps.

First, I told them that this was a vital part of their job and they had to learn it. Second, I sent over the one person in the department who knew the hardware and software inside and out. She was definitely someone they all respected. It took only two days before these people were handling the computer and its programs as if they were born to the job.

STAFFING

Staffing, usually associated with the personnel department, is also one of the most important human resource management activities of all RMs because it often sets the stage for the future effectiveness or failure of their units. There are a number of functions suggested in the literature that are performed by effective RMs during the staffing process. The following examines three of the primary ones.

Developing Job Descriptions

Job descriptions provide an important basis from which to make staffing decisions. If detailed in nature, they contain a general description of the job, examples of work performed, and general qualification requirements that must be possessed by the jobholder. Although RMs usually do not write these descriptions, effective ones do see that they are sufficiently detailed and accurate to allow an easy preliminary screening of applicants.

A job description must be complete, listing all the activities carried out by the jobholder. The description must be clear so that whoever reads it is able to understand the activities to be done and the qualifications necessary to do them. The description must also be concise, providing brief examples of the work and specific job objectives that explain how successful work behavior will be measured.

Interviewing Job Opening Candidates

Most effective RMs like to talk to prospective job candidates before they are hired. This interview can take a number of different forms. Some RMs prefer a highly structured interview in which a series of questions are written down and asked in sequential order. Others prefer a highly unstructured interview in which the two casually talk and the RM tries to formulate an impression about the ability of the candidate to do the job.

The most common type of interview used by effective RMs is a combination structured-unstructured format. The primary reason for formulating questions in advance is to ensure that no important query goes unasked. If more than one person is going to be interviewing the candidate, the effective RM coordinates this activity and works out in advance what each person will discuss with the candidate. In this way, the candidate is not asked the same questions by all the interviewers. When the interviews are over, the questioners can pool their thoughts and provide the best possible judgment for the final staffing decision.

The Staffing Decision

Effective RMs, in conjunction with the personnel department, formulate selection criteria and use these as guides in making the final staffing decision. Some of these criteria are found in the job description: formal education, experience, and so forth. Others are determined on the basis of the interview or background checks, that is, how well does this individual work with others, what are his or her goals, and will the person fit in well in this organization. Quite often these are judgment calls, but if the proper hiring criteria are in place, the RM should find it easier to make an informed decision. One effective manager trusted his intuition in the hiring process:

> Before I hire, I like to talk to the applicant and get an idea of what this person is like. I think I know the type of person who will fit in here. I look for the right chemistry. If it's there, I hire the person; if it's not, I don't. This may sound awfully unsophisticated, but I look to the first part of the hiring process to handle the routine stuff such as experience, training, education, background, and so forth. All of this can be put down on a piece of paper and used to guide me. However, my hiring decision is based heavily on what *isn't* on the piece of paper.

TRAINING AND DEVELOPMENT

Closely related to the staffing function of human resources management is the training and development function. Again, formal training and development are closely associated with the personnel department, but there are a number of activities that effective RMs carry out in this area. The following examines some of the most common training and development activities in which effective RMs are involved.

Orientation

Orientation has overlooked, but important, long-run payoffs. In particular, some organizations have found that new personnel who are not given a realistic orientation are much more likely to leave the organization during the first year than those who are. The orientation is the beginning and, therefore, the most important part of the socialization process of employees. The longer, more intense, and more realistic the orientation, the greater the chance that the new employee will learn the values and overall culture of the organization.

Most orientation programs cover such topics as: the history of the organization and the major services or products being provided; the structure and reporting relationships; personnel rules, policies, and practices; compensation and benefits provided; and the daily routines and regulations. In large organizations, the formal part of this orientation is carried out by the personnel department; in small organizations, the manager may handle this entire function. However, even in large organizations, managers are largely responsible for providing the values and expectations and explaining the culture to new employees under their direction. Here are some guidelines suggested by the literature that would be supported by effective RMs:

1. Orientation should start with the most relevant and useful kinds of information and then proceed to the more general, peripheral types of information.
2. A large percentage of the orientation should provide employees with information related to what supervisors and co-workers are like, should explain how to attain desired work output standards, and should encourage personnel to seek advice and help when they are unsure of how to proceed with a work project.
3. Each new employee (at all levels) should be assigned an experienced person, a mentor, who can provide assistance and encouragement, answer questions, and help the individual get through the first couple of months. This is vital to the employee's socialization process.

4. New workers should be given sufficient time to master their jobs before the demands on them are increased. They should progress a step at a time.

Identifying Training Needs and Implementation Approaches

Managers need to identify training needs and then design the training to meet these needs. For new hires, this is most often done by RMs providing on-the-job training that familiarizes them with the work and how to do it. One of the most common examples is that of walking new employees through the job and then observing them while they perform the job.

If training cannot be done on the job, effective RMs arrange for off-the-job training for their people. This can take a number of different forms. For lower level employees who are operating machinery or equipment, vestibule training is often employed. This training takes place in an environment that simulates the actual workplace. Once the individuals have completed the vestibule training, they can be placed in an actual work setting, where, with some coaching and support from their managers, they are able to perform the job properly.

For management or employee development in areas such as computer programming, communication, and human resource management skills, outside trainers/consultants will be used most often. Whether in-house or outside training is offered, the objective is to provide the participants with education and development that they can take back to the job and use to enhance their effectiveness and eventually benefit the organization.

Some organizations use standard training and development programs for all of their personnel. Others try to tailor the training and development to the needs of the individual. In the latter case, effective RMs identify the types of training and development that their people need and then make sure the necessary programs are provided. In large firms, this may be coordinated under the auspices of the personnel department, but effective RMs take it upon themselves if necessary; in small organizations RMs handle the arrangements on a department-by-department basis. One manager explained:

> I have a budget for providing training to my people, and it's up to me to decide how this will be done. I have to handle everything. Usually I get outside

trainers to handle the human relations material because I don't think we have anyone in-house who can do this training effectively. However, for on-the-job training to learn the job initially and work more efficiently, I do a lot of that myself. By walking around, seeing who has a problem mastering the technical side of their job, I have a pretty good idea of what is needed. Then I help them do it or I assign someone who can help.

Meanwhile, informal training such as coaching and counseling is personally handled on a day-to-day basis by RMs. This often takes the form of mentoring.

The Mentoring Approach to Training and Developing

A mentor coaches, counsels, teaches, and assists someone. Mentoring is particularly important to young employees. Many effective RMs make it a point to assign a mentor to each of their people and serve as one themselves. Mentors show their people the ropes, explain how to use networks effectively (see Chapter 7), introduce their charges to people who can help their careers, and are available should problems develop or advice be needed.

These relationships yield high returns. Those with a mentor are more likely to get ahead than their counterparts without mentors. They also seem to be more satisfied with their career progress and the pleasure they derive from their work.

Effective RMs in our study not only provided mentoring to others, but they had mentors of their own. The effect of this mentoring process is spelled out in the following example:

Mentoring is important to success. I go out of my way to provide it to my favorite young people coming up, even though we don't have a formal mentoring system. To me it's nothing more than a form of training and development, with a heavy sprinkling of realism. I try to tell those I'm mentoring the way it really is in this company. I want them to know the things to do and things not to do. For example, networking is important but if you try to network with the wrong person you may end up being tagged as "over-aggressive," and this can hurt your career. I try to teach my people how to avoid these problems. A lot of a young person's success in this company is knowing what to do and how to do it. A mentor can help ensure that the person he's helping out knows these things.

Career Development

Mentoring is just one of the ways in which effective RMs help subordinates and themselves with their careers. Another method is helping subordinates master their jobs so that they are ready to move on to other career opportunities. One manager made this distinction:

> One of the things I look for in a promotable person is competence. Does the individual know his job and does he do it well? If so, I think the person is ready to move up; if not, perhaps the individual has topped out, reached his level of incompetence, like in the Peter Principle.

Building a resume or record that shows that one is ready to move up in a career path is a useful strategy. Effective RMs help out here by encouraging their people to do things such as keep a "hero" file. Every reward, recommendation, performance evaluation, or memo related to the person's work output is kept in this file. It can become important ammunition to support merit pay and promotion considerations. One manager explained:

> Whenever one of my people does something particularly noteworthy, I make it a point to send this individual a memo. It doesn't necessarily go in the person's official personnel file, but I expect the individual to hang on to it. In this way, even if these people decide to leave the organization, this file can be used to support their job application. A hero file is important because sometimes you need to blow your own horn and be able to back it up with solid evidence.

Effective RMs also assist their subordinates with career development by helping them identify career goals and formulate a plan for attaining these goals. Especially in large companies, this activity is often supported through the efforts of the personnel department. In medium and small firms, effective RMs often take this task upon themselves.

There are a number of ways that career development can be done. One is by having subordinates set forth those goals they would like to attain during the next five or ten years. The manager and the subordinate examine how realistic these goals are both organizationally (is the career path one that is in step with company practices?) and personally (does the individual have the ability to reach these goals?). Then they discuss the subordinate's career path and how to attain his goals. The result is a short-range career plan that can be updated annually.

I try to help my people put together a career plan by focusing both on what they want to do and what the needs of the organization are likely to be over the next five to ten years. If someone is a very successful salesperson and wants to move into the management ranks, obviously the individual will have to be promoted to local and then regional sales manager. The first areas of consideration are: what are the requirements to be promoted to a local sales manager's position; how often are there openings at this level; and how many people are currently in line? This gives us an idea of both where and how fast this salesperson can move. If the individual can expect to be promoted to this position within two years, and that is in line with her career plan, everything is fine. We will discuss the matter again when the promotion is at hand. If the person has little chance of getting the promotion or it will take longer than she wants to wait, we consider what other career moves are available to the individual and which of these is acceptable. We then begin discussing this new career path. You know, it's a lot of fun helping people work through their career plan. It makes me feel I am really helping them and I know it helps them get ahead.

A FINAL WORD

We found that human resource management activities are very important to effective RMs. They ranked second behind communication in their relative relationship to RM effectiveness. Interestingly, however, they ranked last in the relative strength of relationship with successful RMs, and in the comparative analysis, the top third of successful RMs did less of these activities than the bottom third. This finding—that effective RMs give considerable attention to human resource activities but successful RMs do not—has very significant implications for today's organizations. For example, what does it say for those who believe in a human resource management approach, and its effectiveness, but want to get ahead? Pragmatically, our findings indicate that they could better spend their efforts on networking if they want to be promoted as quickly as possible. On the other hand, our data clearly show that those who take a human resource approach are more effective than those who give relatively more attention to networking. A major challenge facing organizations in the near future is to align formal reward systems (promotion, at least) with the *effective* contributions of RMs. The next, and last, chapter will examine these implications and challenges in more depth.

9 CLOSURE AND A POINT OF DEPARTURE

In this final chapter we will review the ground we've covered, take stock, and see where the results of our investigation of RMs have led us. From the beginning, we set out to answer three basic questions:

1. What do real managers do?
2. What do successful real managers do?
3. What do effective real managers do?

Now, in this last chapter we will add a fourth question:

4. What do real managers who are successful *and* effective do?

SUMMARY OF WHERE WE ARE

Our study of real managers provided considerable data about the activities that RMs do and in what relative proportions they do them. In particular, we found that real managers engage in traditional management activities (consisting of behaviors related to planning, decisionmaking, and controlling); routine communication activities (consisting of behaviors associated with exchanging routine information and handling

157

paperwork); human resource management activities (consisting of behaviors descriptive of motivating/reinforcing, disciplining/punishing, managing conflict, staffing, and training/developing); and networking activities (consisting of behaviors associated with socializing/politicking and interacting with outsiders).

We found that all four of these RM activities were done relatively frequently. Traditional management came in at 32 percent, routine communications at 29 percent, human resource management at 20 percent, and networking at 19 percent. These results verify the popular assumption of the importance of traditional management and routine communication activities. In addition, however, it was discovered that RMs give considerable emphasis to human resource management and networking in their day-to-day activities.

We found evidence from several analyses that successful RMs give relatively different emphasis to managerial activities than do their unsuccessful counterparts. In particular, we found through statistical analysis that successful RMs did significantly more of the networking activity. The other activities were not significantly related to successful RMs. In addition, the comparative descriptive analysis revealed that the top third of successful RMs were doing a great deal more networking and slightly more communicating activities than the bottom third. Importantly, in this comparative analysis, we found that the successful RMs were doing relatively less human resource and traditional management activities than the bottom third.

When we rank ordered the relative strengths of the managerial activities' relationship to RM success, we saw that, as with the other two analyses, the networking activity had the strongest relative relationship with successful RMs. Although human resource activities fared somewhat better and communication activities somewhat worse in this relative strength of relationship analysis than in the comparative analysis, all three analyses (statistical, comparative, and relative strength of relationship) had a common, revealing finding. Multiple analysis methods found what many observers, both inside and out, of the management scene have suspected for years—the way to get ahead and be successful in organizations is to give a lot of attention to networking activities (that is, socializing/politicking and interacting with outsiders).

The third question of what do effective RMs do is the most important, but most difficult, to answer. Communication activities had the strongest relative relationship to managerial effectiveness, followed, in turn, by human resource and traditional management activities. Interestingly, networking had the weakest relationship to managerial effectiveness. This effectiveness analysis result, of course, is in stark contrast to the success analysis result. Networking has the strongest relationship with successful RMs but the weakest relationship with effective RMs. Communication and human resource management activities have the strongest relationships with effective RMs.

In summary, we found that managers are doing the activities generally acknowledged over the years (with the possible addition of human resource activities and, especially, networking) but, importantly, the successful RMs are not necessarily doing the same activities as the effective ones. In other words, the successful managers do not appear to be the same as the effective managers. However, before closing our study of RMs, one lingering question remains: what about those RMs who are both successful *and* effective?

SUCCESSFUL *AND* EFFECTIVE REAL MANAGERS

Throughout the book we have made a clear distinction between successful RMs and effective RMs. In the last phase of the analysis we decided to look at the RMs who are both successful *and* effective. After all, these managers have it all. They are successful in terms of relatively fast promotions in their respective organizations, and they are effective in that they have satisfied and committed subordinates and are judged to run high-performing units. However, given that successful RMs were found to be quite different than effective RMs, we did not expect to find many in our data base who were both successful and effective. We were right—there were very few RMs who met criteria for both success and effectiveness. Nevertheless, we think it is important to take a closer look at these successful and effective RMs.

How We Determined the Successful and Effective RMs

Our sample of 178 RMs gave us enough data to calculate the success index defined in Chapter 3 and the effectiveness index defined in Chapter 4. Because we used only the top third of each sample in our previous analyses, we applied the same rule here. Thus, in order to determine those RMs that were both successful and effective, we took the top third of successful RMs and the top third of effective RMs and identified those that were common to both groups. We found fifteen RMs who were both successful and effective according to this procedure (see Figure 9–1).

What Do Successful and Effective RMs Do?

From our previous analyses on successful and effective RMs, we found that successful RMs are not generally the same as effective RMs. As stated in Chapters 3 and 4, we found successful RMs do relatively more networking activities and effective RMs do relatively more communicating and human resource management activities. However, for the few cases where RMs are both successful *and* effective ($N = 15$ of our sample of 178 RMs), their activities are almost identical to RMs as a whole. The successful *and* effective RMs do not seem to do the activities of either the successful or effective RMs or some unique hybrid of the two; instead, successful *and* effective RMs do activities that are identical to RMs in general.

Figure 9–2 shows the breakdown of each of the major activities for the 15 successful *and* effective RMs. When compared to Figure 2–3 which showed the breakdown of all 248 RMs observed in the study,

Figure 9-1.   Determination of Successful *and* Effective RMs ($N = 15$).

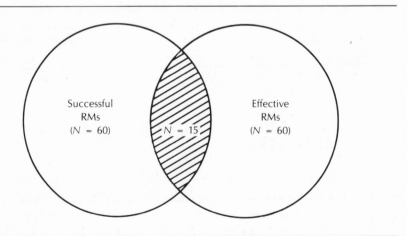

Successful
RMs
($N = 60$)

$N = 15$

Effective
RMs
($N = 60$)

Figure 9–2. Comparison of Successful *and* Effective Real Managers' Activities with the Activities of All Real Managers.

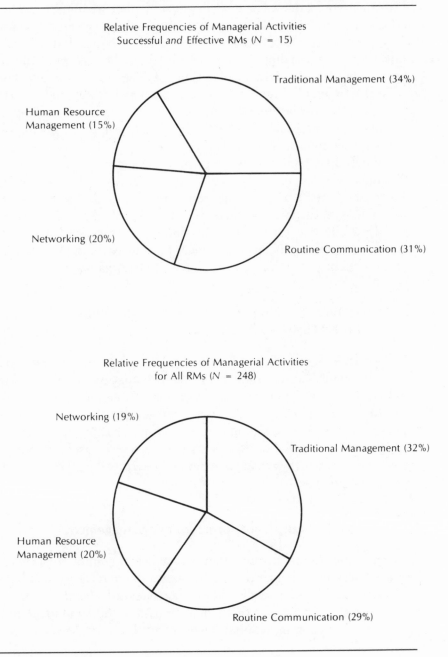

Relative Frequencies of Managerial Activities
Successful *and* Effective RMs (*N* = 15)

Traditional Management (34%)

Human Resource
Management (15%)

Networking (20%)

Routine Communication (31%)

Relative Frequencies of Managerial Activities
for All RMs (*N* = 248)

Networking (19%)

Traditional Management (32%)

Human Resource
Management (20%)

Routine Communication (29%)

the relative frequencies are almost the same. This was also true of the sample of 178 RMs used in the present analysis.

In other words, those few RMs in our study that are both successful and effective are not really distinctive from real managers in general. They use a fairly balanced approach to their activities. This, in and of itself, may be revealing. It says that in order to be successful *and* effective, none of the activities can be ignored. The previous chapters on traditional management, communication, networking, and human resource management pointed out that all these activities are important, and now empirically, at least with these fifteen RMs, the importance of all activities is verified.

Any definitive conclusions concerning the successful *and* effective RMs must be tempered by the small number of RMs that were found to meet the criteria. Of more interest, and potentially having greater implications, is the fact that there were so few RMs that are both successful and effective. Once again, this finding that successful managers are *not* the same as effective managers has far-reaching implications for the present and future performance of our organizations.

HOW OUR FINDINGS FIT WITH MODERN MANAGEMENT THINKING

Using our findings of what RMs do as a point of departure, we reviewed a host of popular books aimed at practicing managers to examine how the four RM activities corresponded with modern management thinking. We found that the traditional management, human resources management, routine communication, and networking activities not only generally fit well, but these activities can also be useful as a common base from which we can reference and interpret the other currently popular approaches.

The Fit with "Transformational" Management

One currently popular theme in the management literature advocated by Bernard Bass and others is that performance-based reward systems are old fashioned. The argument is that traditional rewards characterize transactional management, and that a new, transformational management is needed to replace transactional management. Traditional transactional management is based on the manager identifying or creating subordinates' needs and arranging consequences to satisfy those needs in exchange for work-related performance. In the new transformational management, on the other hand, the manager sensitizes subordinates to superordinate goals and such higher order needs as self-actualization. This transformational management does not rely on traditional reward systems, but on charismatic (inspirational) leadership. For example, in practice, subordinates might be inspired to believe that they are at the cutting edge of a great organizational change for the better—that they are the greatest or best or most capable employees in the world, and that the changes will help them reach their full potential as contributing members of a better society.

To bring about a transformational approach in real work settings requires that the manager be able to sensitize subordinates to the importance of the superordinate goals, demonstrate that the goals can be achieved by the subordinates, and provide credibility. The success of the transformational approach hinges on the manager's skill as a communicator to sensitize and to lead human resources (subordinates, peers, and even superiors). A skilled communicator and human resource manager under the transformational approach can provide positive reinforcement and confidence and can deliberately alter organizational culture in a positive way. The correspondence with our study of RMs: these two key elements in transformational management (communication and human resource management) are also the two major contributing activities to RM effectiveness.

The Fit with "Radical" Management

S.A. Culbert and J.J. McDonough cite motivation as one of the most misused concepts in management in their "radical management" approach. They claim that in its perverted form, motivation is defined as: (1) getting someone to want what the manager wants; (2) arranging reward/punishment consequences to produce performance demanded by the manager; and (3) forcing recalcitrants to perform when the manager has no knowledge of the reasons for recalcitrant behavior. Radical management is based on the premise that *trust* is motivating and that organizations that can achieve high levels of trust among their members are likely to be the most successful.

Although this trust-based approach connotes altruism, this is not an entirely altruistic approach. It could be based on the question, "Have you ever bought anything from, or had very much to do with, someone you didn't trust?" At the risk of oversimplifying, the approach includes three levels in its implementation. The first, counseling, consists of developing an accommodation between the organization member's personal needs and the organizational needs, and getting others in the environment to recognize that the niche the person has chosen to fill contributes significantly to the organization. This amounts to a constructive advising/counseling/negotiating process (but is not management by objectives in disguise). To do their part effectively, managers must be secure enough not to be threatened by subordinates' selected goals and by the niches, strategies, or means they select to achieve those goals. It is here, again, that the communication and human resource management activities of RMs become essential. RM networking activities are also helpful if the subordinate is to be included in one of the manager's networks.

The second level of implementation in radical management is team building. This focuses on helping people to recognize that the niches others have chosen to fill also contribute significantly to the organization. This activity often occurs when the RM performs the role of peacemaker in the managing conflict dimension of the human resource management activity (listening to and resolving grievances among subordinates and peers). This role is aimed at developing interpersonal tolerance and understanding among subordinate members of the work unit. The fit with RM communication and human resource management activities is clear.

The third level of radical management, brokering, addresses two objectives. The first is to develop advocacy for the work unit, or organization, among other work units (for example, to get other work units to value the positive contribution of the manager's work unit). The second objective is to develop the most productive correspondence between the niches subordinates select to fill and the expectations of the client environment (for example, to get everyone in the work unit to adjust their niches to "satisfice" the expectations of the manager's boss or outside clients, and to adjust those expectations to fit whatever the work unit does best). This part of the radical management process brings all of the RM activities into play (that is, communicating, human resource management, traditional management, and networking).

It should be obvious in this radical management approach that managers need to be secure and mature with their subordinates. If they feel threatened by their subordinates' contributions, it will not be possible for them to implement the approach successfully. For example, a competitive or subservient leader-subordinate relationship precludes trust and renders the full potential of the approach unattainable. Managers who believe that their subordinates are inferior to themselves are simply not ready to implement the third step—they aren't ready to "sell" their work unit.

This radical management approach fits with our four major RM activities, and with our findings relative to RM success and effectiveness. More specifically, effective RMs appear to be implementing the counseling and team-building steps (that is, communicating and human resource management activities), and successful RMs appear to be emphasizing the brokering and team-building steps (that is, networking activities).

The Fit with "Feedback"

Current management literature advocates the use of objective performance feedback to enhance employee job satisfaction and motivation potential. For example, high achievers need immediate feedback. Feedback provides valued information, recognition, and attention for employees. Applied to goal setting, feedback can be used to correct deviations from a goal or from the manager's performance expectations. Also, feedback may be a positive reinforcer in and of itself.

Feedback can be built into the job design so that employees can immediately know how they are doing. For example, this might be used in semiautomated test equipment in critical assembly-line alignment or adjustment processes. It is used in video display terminal (VDT) tasks where the operator is informed of errors and omissions with on-screen feedback, and end-of-day or week tallies of overall errors or output. In addition to feedback from the job itself, employees can also receive feedback from their supervisors. Just as employees dislike manipulation, they chafe at having their existence ignored. In many cultures ostracism is used as formal punishment. In our modern organizations we do not formally build in such punishment, but by not providing personal, objective feedback to employees, we create a similar situation. Lack of feedback often has serious consequences and often occurs because of the constraints of time and size.

We found that successful RMs use feedback liberally in their networking activities—to pay their debts, to furnish information, and to reinforce the behavior of other members of the network for supporting them. If they fail to do this they are likely to be expelled from their respective networks. Effective RMs provide feedback in the course of their communication and human resource activities with subordinates. Successful and effective managers know that positive feedback provides positive results, both in getting ahead for successful RMs and getting the job done and satisfying subordinates for effective RMs. Negative feedback given in anger, in contempt, or with the hope that the subordinate or peer who receives it will fail is difficult to disguise and only serves to humiliate and alienate. Effective managers give performance feedback that is positive, immediate, graphic, and specific.

The Fit with "Organizational Culture"

A great deal is being written currently on the subject of organizational or corporate culture. The subject is so popular that at least one senior-level manager is known to have ordered his corporate staff to "create a corporate culture by next week." An organizational culture consists of the shared understandings, norms, values, attitudes, and beliefs within an organization. It has also been expressed as the organization's basic values, philosophy, and financial, technical, and human concerns. It is reflected in the organization's stories, humor, role models, symbols, ceremonies, concepts of time, beliefs about human nature, responsiveness to the external environment, and performance expectations for its employees. When new employees are taken into the organization, they undergo a socialization process in which they learn the values, beliefs, and behaviors that are expected of them. One outcome of this process is that the organizational members develop shared interpretations of work-related events.

In short, an organizational culture is very much like an organizational "personality," and like a human personality, it is comprised of a constellation of traits, gathered over a long developmental period. Many of these cultural traits of organizations are useful and necessary; some are not. For example, on the positive side, caution in high-risk, high-value decisions is both useful and necessary. However, when the organization carries that caution to excess, such as ceasing to respond to its competitive environment, the element of caution in the organizational culture may not be useful. Expectations of infallibility in a corporate culture often include severe penalties for failure. In such organizations, risk taking and initiative are often extinguished.

One demanding RM problem is to recognize which characteristics of the organization's culture are useful and which must be changed so that the organization can remain or become effective. As with human personality, unless the organization recognizes and accepts its need to change, (as for example, did the Chrysler Corporation), those seeking to alter the corporate personality or culture do so at their own peril. The process of shaping organizational culture is a variant of the organizational development process and must be done gradually and with care.

Can managers really shape their organizational cultures? As the social tapestry outside the organization changes and new generations of employees join the organization, their expectations regarding working conditions, wages and salaries, and performance-related rewards differ from those of the earlier generation of employees, often resulting in conflict. This levies a requirement for managers to develop an accommodation between the organizational and the new social culture in the same way that they develop an accommodation between existing physical facilities and procedures with new technology. It means that organizational culture is constantly in a gradual state of change.

Let's see how the four RM activities fit with such an analysis of organizational culture. How can a manager shape organizational culture to establish a success-oriented, rather than mediocre or failure-oriented, environment? RMs intending to do this would have to alter the organization's basic values, its philosophy, and its financial, technical, and human concerns. They can do this by changing shared understandings, norms, values, attitudes, and beliefs within their organization. They could translate these intentions into actions by adding to or replacing the organization's stories, humor, role models, symbols, ceremonies, concepts of time, beliefs about human nature, responsiveness to the external environment, or performance expectations for employees.

All RMs do the above actions in their everyday activities. However, they are probably unaware of their effect on the organization culture. For example, the successes and failures of RMs (as well as those of their peers, bosses, and subordinates) add to organizational stories. When RMs convey their values and expectations by their activities (communication, human resource management, traditional management, and networking), they alter shared norms, values, attitudes, beliefs, and understandings. Even their inactivity has such effects. Each RM behavioral event either reinforces the status quo or is an antecedent for future change.

Simply stated, the real organization is always in a state of flux or change. How RMs affect that change hinges on their day-to-day activities.

RMs who exert positive influences are those who are effective, whose activities are especially related to communication and human resource management. However, those RMs who are *not* effective also shape the organizational culture. When they are deliberately destructive and counterproductive, they shape it negatively. Fortunately, most organizations are resilient and survivable. In good economic conditions, organizations survive in spite of, rather than because of, the way they are managed. Yet, in tight economic times, or even more pronounced recently, because of global competition from the Japanese and a growing list of others, U.S. organizations will have to devote more attention to the positive, effective activities of RMs that shape organizational culture.

The Fit with New Ideas about Organization

We often ask ourselves how serious workplace misunderstandings and high levels of conflict or nonresponsiveness can occur when "everyone knows" the importance of the task at hand. L.G. Bolman and T.E. Deal have recently described four perspectives, or frameworks, about organizations—a kind of safari through the organizational theory "jungle." The frameworks include: (1) the rational systems perspective, which focuses on the fit between the organizations' goals, roles, technology, purpose, structure, and environment; (2) the human resource perspective, which focuses on relationships between the organization and its people; their needs, skills, and culture; and the mechanisms for maximizing mutual benefit; (3) the political perspective, which emphasizes obtaining or controlling scarce resources, influence, power, conflict, and conflict resolution; and (4) the symbolic perspective, which emphasizes how stories, legends, symbols, rituals, and ceremonies give meaning to the organization.

When organizational members are exclusively focused on *different* frameworks, it is virtually impossible for them to communicate. For example, an organization member with a human resource-based perspective (for example, a participative management approach) would be regarded with suspicion or contempt by an organization member with a purely politically oriented perspective. The latter would believe that power is the major factor affecting subordinate performance, and human resource activity is important only to the extent that it controls confrontation and conflict, or to the extent that it contributes to obtaining more power. From a human resource perspective, the political orientation is immorally manipulative and disregards the concept that employees want to do the "right" thing in as autonomous an environment as possible (for example, people are more productive under a Theory Y approach than under Theory X).

Another example would be a situation where a symbolically based explanation is offered to explain current events in the organization. For example, the union is taking a firm stand in current labor negotiations because the history of labor negotiations in the organization is replete with activist union heroes and management villains, and an adversarial relationship between management and labor is accepted as fact. Not to be outdone, management has equally adversarial stories to tell about the union. This kind of explanation for opposition at the bargaining table can be frustrating to union or management negotiators who are seeking explanations and solutions in a rational systems frame of reference. Clearly, establishing a common ground for negotiation, in the face of such mutually inflammatory perspectives, is a difficult task, one that is not achievable without a keen perception of the underlying perspectives and the real issues.

Bolman and Deal claim that each of the four perspectives, or frames, can contribute strongly to the organization, and that organizations are most effective when the perspectives are balanced with each other (when they are "aligned"). The four perspectives also correspond to specific management functions and concerns. For example, the rational systems perspective, which they term the "structural frame," deals with providing direction for organizational goals, defining the organizational structure, and "task accomplishment." The human resource perspective addresses using human resources sensitivity to human needs effectively. The political perspective encompasses resource allocation, conflict, and strategies to obtain power. The symbolic perspective covers shaping the organizational culture (shared values, symbols, and cohesion).

Comparing these new ideas of organization with the four RM activities, we find some fit. The rational systems perspective is basically covered by RM traditional management and communication activities. The human resource perspective directly translates to RM human resource activities. The political perspective also directly translates to RM networking activities. Thus, directly observable RM activities correlate with the rational systems, human resource, and political perspectives of organization. By definition, however, the symbolic perspective does not correspond with the directly observable RM activities. The discussion in the last section on organizational culture is more appropriate for the symbolic perspective.

The Fit with More Conventional Management Ideas

Although the RM activities seem to fit well with state-of-the-art and non-traditional management ideas discussed so far, it is also useful to review the relevance of RM activities to the more conventional approaches recommended in current books aimed at management practitioners.

Most of this conventional literature focuses on common concerns shared by all employees. For example, all employees want to know why they are participating in their organizations. What is the significance of being in this particular organization that is distinctively different from being elsewhere? The organization should have a fully developed philosophy, but after the philosophy statement has been made, maintaining its credibility becomes a full-time job. When that credibility begins to wane, employee concern reappears and is reflected in the employee's organizational commitment. The RM, who does not deal in philosophy, can use the day-to-day communication and human resource management activities to help overcome such employee concerns.

A second concern is with the organizational expectations for employees. Conflicting goals generate considerable concern. New employees prefer clear goals to uncertain ones, but older employees, even managers, having gained experience and sensitivity to become more observant, are outraged and feel betrayed when stated organizational goals and philosophy and actual managerial behavior appear to be incongruent and contradictory.

The literature recognizes at least six types of organizational goals: (1) stated goals—the announced goals of the organization or management, which serve as performance targets for employees; (2) stereotype goals—the goals commonly regarded as socially acceptable and reputable; (3) existing goals—the combined goals of the organization's members that are part of the organizational culture; (4) honorific "boy scout goals"—the goals that impute admirable qualities to the organization; (5) taboo goals—real but covert organizational goals; and (6) repressed goals—real, actively, perhaps unconsciously pursued, goals that contradict the organization's self-image and values. If organizational participants seek truth in this melange of goals they can only find "double-speak" in six flavors. The managing conflict part of RM human resource management activities is especially pertinent to this concern. Another concern evolves around employees wanting to know how they're doing; in other words, they need feedback. They also want to know how their activities will benefit them, and who will provide what kinds of help when they need it. To respond to these specific concerns, RMs do communication and human resource management activities. Although these concerns could be addressed with traditional management activities, such an approach would not convey the personal interest and credibility of the manager. This example should help put into perspective the reasons why the more effective RMs emphasize communication and human resource management activities over traditional management activities.

To elaborate still further, Table 9-1 offers a sampling of the key concepts and courses of action discussed in current conventional books for practitioners. We have marked which of the four RM activities we believe are most essential to do each of these recommended concepts or courses of action effectively.

Interestingly, we find that our estimate of essential RM activities appears across the sample list of current concepts and courses of action in the same relative order or frequency as our empirical findings for their relative contribution to RM effectiveness (that is, communication, human resource management, traditional management, and networking). Table 9-1 shows that, in light of the current management literature, be it avant garde or simply seeking modest improvement in performance, effective RMs need to do a great deal of communication and human resource management activities. Our evidence indicates that effective RMs are doing precisely these activities. The implication is that less effective managers, who are more tightly focused on traditional planning, decisionmaking, and controlling activities, as well as socializing/politicking and interacting with outsider activities, are not utilizing the full potential of their human resources.

It is ironic that the justification for a narrow traditional management focus is to maximize productivity. Because of human factors, that formula turns out to be inadequate. What we now call "traditional" management practice was, a century ago, an evolutionary step prompted by economic necessity—a need for greater efficiency and less waste of resources. Now, however, managers in many competing nations have a clearer understanding than we do that people are also resources, and that they can make greater differences in productivity than can refinements

Table 9–1. Concepts and Courses of Action Recommended in Current Conventional Literature Fit to RM Activities.

| | Relevant RM Activities | | | |
	Human Resource Management	Routine Communication	Networking	Traditional Management
Concept/Course of Action				
Adding value	X	X		X
Addressing real underlying issues	X	X	X	X
Charismatic leadership	X		X	
Consequence analysis				X
Defusing tension	X	X	X	
Developing promotability among subordinates	X		X	
Managing by motivation	X			
Effective teams	X			
Expressing expectations	X	X		X
Feedback	X	X		
Legitimizing leadership ability and credibility				X
Listening skills	X	X		
Matching employee personal and professional goals	X	X		
Not "routinizing to death"	X		X	
Performance-based reward	X			X
Quality circles	X	X		
Reinforcing interdependence	X		X	
Specifying productive work behaviors	X	X		X
Transforming intentions into results	X	X		X
Trust-based management	X	X	X	
Using lateral relationships	X	X	X	

in traditional management approaches. For example, the Japanese give top priority to a formal strategy of human resource management. They have implemented human resource techniques such as participative management (for example, quality circles) and overall human resource policies (for example, life-time employment) while most American organizations are still just talking about them. We are once again prompted by economic necessity to greater efficiency and fewer wasted resources. We can't afford to waste human resource potential; effective RMs are taking it upon themselves to maximize these activities.

MANAGEMENT SKILLS NEEDED NOW AND IN THE FUTURE

Our research shows that successful RMs and effective RMs do activities differently than their less successful and effective counterparts. These activities are trainable skills. We will now discuss how these equate to current training and development needs and project implications for these skills into the future.

The Need for Communication Skills

As we've emphasized throughout this book, we empirically found and therefore conclude that effective managers need to be effective communicators. They need to know more than how to write and verbalize understandable instructions. They need to understand the effects of what they write and say, including the implications of writing or saying too much or too little. For example, writing warnings to subordinates to document poor performance, or formalizing a specific objective in written form, may be necessary and proper. However, writing just to establish a "paper trail," devastates trust. So does the infamous "poisonous memo" used to document a one-sided interpretation or position. RMs should be sensitive to the effects of formal written memos. There are few things more uninspiring, or more hateful, than written memos. Managers who put too much information in writing eventually dull the ear of the receiver. Organization members eventually disregard nagging communicators, regardless of their rank.

Listening skills are equally important. Messages are not what they always appear to be. The manager's style is not necessarily an indicator of his or her listening skill. Autocratic managers might be expected to be poor listeners because they believe that it is the subordinate's role to listen and comply. More human-oriented managers might be expected to be more empathetic listeners. The traditional management literature tends to give an autocratic management style negative connotations. Yet the autocratic manager may indeed be a sensitive, perceptive listener. Similarly, we tend to make positive attributions about human-oriented managers (that is, they are empathetic listeners), when in fact they may be insensitive and unresponsive listeners.

For example, many RMs have issued standing invitations to their subordinates to visit and discuss problems. One such manager listened to a valid grievance for two hours, took copious notes, then did nothing to change the situation. The subordinate was more dissatisfied after the interview than before. The RM's listening objective was to let the subordinate vent his feelings and to gather as much information about the subordinate as possible. Two-way communication never occurred. The manager didn't interrupt. He was courteous to the subordinate and gave all of the return cues to indicate that he was paying attention. Was he a skillful listener?

This brings us to the purpose of skillful listening and its positive or negative effect on the manager's general performance. RMs who are passive, insensitive, or unresponsive may be good listeners, but they don't necessarily translate information and intentions into action. They simply adjust their listening behavior to the management style to which they've become accustomed. In contrast, RMs who do translate information and intentions into action also fit their listening behavior into their management style. The point is that being a good listener does not guarantee being an effective manager. However, being a poor listener virtually guarantees being an ineffective manager, because managers who are poor listeners simply have less information with which to work.

The RM who is a skillful listener can also hear the messages in the background:

- What do senders see as the real issues that affect them?
- Why do senders fantasize achievements that they haven't accomplished (that is, confuse their intent to do things with actually doing them)?
- Why do senders name drop or maintain a high or low profile?
- What is their self-image?
- What are their aspirations?

- What is their sense of time?
- What are their priorities?
- Does their home life complement or conflict with their work?
- Where can accommodations be made to better suit the employee to the job?
- What is the organizational culture?
- How is organizational change occurring—its direction, its speed?
- Are any good things happening in the work environment?

Some of this information can be obtained by direct questioning, while some must be obtained unobtrusively. Listening skills take practice and time, but the alternative is more uncertainty and risk. Effective RMs have these communicating skills.

The Need for Interpersonal Skills

We devoted chapters to networking and human resources management and the way in which these activities are actually done by RMs. However, just reading about them is insufficient. Networking and human resource management activities require skills in developing and maintaining productive interpersonal relationships. For example, the RM who is a loner is categorically excluded from networking.

Our analysis shows that RMs who focus on traditional management activities, to the exclusion of the other three activity areas, are both less effective and less successful. We could infer causes for the apparent fixation that some managers have with traditional methods: they may be acting out of habit, or they may be avoiding activities demanding interpersonal skills. Traditional management activities, particularly where quantitative planning, decisionmaking, and controlling methods can be applied, are often more certain than the other human resource management, communication, and networking activities. Managers with strong needs for certainty (low tolerance for ambiguity) tend to concentrate on such traditional activities. Traditional management activities can often be done in private, where no one can see the manager struggle. The other RM activities are usually done spontaneously, always with an audience (bosses, subordinates, peers, or outsiders) to witness one's mistakes. Interpersonal skills always have to be exercised with other people; effective managers need these skills.

The Need for Stress Management Skills

Nearly all real managers live in stressful environments. In the normal course of doing their jobs, they experience high levels of ambiguity and often try to change organizations and people resistant to change. Feelings of frustration are common. In recent years, stress has emerged as a pervasive condition in modern organizational life.

Among the causes of stress are: (1) responsibility for the performance or the welfare of others; (2) lack of involvement in decisions that affect the person experiencing stress; (3) crowded, noisy, uncomfortable working conditions; (4) organizational work and change; and (5) receiving performance evaluations. Stress is not automatically bad, but it can adversely affect physical and mental health as well as work performance.

Individual resistance to stress depends on how people perceive the cause of stress and on the kind of social support they receive. How they maintain their health (for example, exercise, diet, smoking, or use of alcohol) and their resistance to disease also affect resistance to stress.

Interestingly, the things that effective RMs do also serve to manage stress among their subordinates. For example, they give subordinates as much discretion as they can to make their own decisions. They adjust reward systems to be based on performance and regarded as fair. They encourage communication. They are receptive to subordinates giving input regarding the decisions that will affect them.

Skills Needed in the Future

No revolutionary new skills seem needed for the near future. We anticipate that the demands on the skills we've discussed above will intensify. Emerging nations, especially in the Far East, have been quick to adopt human resource management, but worker demands and expectations have lagged far begind. High technology has become easily exportable for production by minimally skilled workers overseas. Very recently, Chinese automobile workers earned about $1 per day, while their U.S. counterparts earned about $100 per day. Emerging nations will continue to follow this pattern. The net result will be that our present problems with labor costs will also intensify over the near future, as new nations join the labor market.

A major part of our problem lies in our cultural values concerning productivity and competence. For example, how much should employees produce, how knowledgeable should they be about their jobs, how receptive should they be to retraining? Changing perceptions and expectations will require changes both in organizational and general societal values. To effect such change, RMs will need to have a broad base of knowledge and skills on which to draw. They will have to view situations from many perspectives and be sensitive to the effects of their own behavior. They will need to be courageous enough to test themselves and to retain their optimism. We think that RMs will respond well to these challenges.

The Need for Skills to Manage Change

One of the manager's most important functions for the future is to introduce and manage change. Planning change and preparing, intervening, and restructuring work and the organization are only part of the change process. As in athletics, music, and romance, timing is everything: knowing when to act is also a key part of the management change process.

Under the most favorable conditions, change requires traditional management activities—to plan, decide, and control. In addition, effective management of change requires communication and human resource management activities—to minimize the threat of change and prepare others to accept and support the change—and networking activities—to provide supplemental resources when they are needed. Obviously there is some overlap among these RM activities. For example, when personally and organizationally essential routines, such as communication channels, are removed, they must be replaced with equally or more effective ones. The control aspect of this task falls under traditional management. However, resolving consequent interpersonal problems among peers or subordinates, during the implementation phase, would fall under networking, communication, and human resource management activities. These overlapping requirements point to the need for hybrid or eclectic managers in the future.

A FINAL WORD

In our study of real managers, we found what they do and how successful and effective ones do things differently from their unsuccessful and ineffective counterparts. We were most impressed by the awakened spirit among RMs to do better, to become excellent. For too long, the formulas for achieving managerial excellence, at least in modern America, have focused on technology and such functional skills as marketing, finance, and production. Our study of RMs suggests that it may be much simpler. We found that RMs are doing the activities we have known about (that is, the traditional management and communication activities) for years. But, importantly, they are also doing more—human resource management and networking activities. It is these latter two, overlooked sets of activities and their relationships that may be the key to managerial excellence. Resolving if not eliminating, our discovered difference between successful and effective real managers may be the key challenge for true managerial excellence in the critical years ahead.

SUPPLEMENTAL READINGS
AND REFERENCES

The text of *Real Managers* contains no specific references or footnotes because, except in the few cases noted, it presents original data. We also wanted to keep it as readable as possible. There are, nevertheless, a number of relevant background as well as directly relevant references for the interested reader. The foundation for our study comes primarily from social learning theory. The most comprehensive and widely recognized source for social learning theory can be found in Albert Bandura, *Social Learning Theory*, (Englewood Cliffs, N.J.: Prentice-Hall, 1977).

More specific application of social learning and accompanying observational techniques to leadership and managerial behavior can be found in Fred Luthans, "Leadership: A Proposal for a Social Learning Theory Base and Observational and Functional Analysis Techniques to Measure Leader Behavior," in *Crosscurrents in Leadership*, ed. James G. Hunt and Lars L. Larson (Carbondale: Southern Illinois University Press, 1979), pp. 201–208.

Luthans and Tim R.V. Davis, of Cleveland State University, published a number of articles giving further details on a social learning approach, that was used as the point of departure and perspective for the present study. None of these articles, however, contained data from the present study. These include the following:

179

Tim R.V. Davis and Fred Luthans, "Leadership Re-Examined: A Behavioral Approach," *Academy of Management Review* 4, no. 2 (June 1979): 237–48.

Fred Luthans and Tim R.V. Davis, "Behavioral Self-Management: The Missing Link in Managerial Effectiveness," *Organizational Dynamics* 18, no. 1 (Summer 1979): 42–60.

Tim R.V. Davis and Fred Luthans, "Managers in Action: A New Look at Their Behavior and Operating Modes," *Organizational Dynamics* 9, no. 1 (Summer 1980): 64–80.

Tim R.V. Davis and Fred Luthans, "A Social Learning Approach to Organizational Behavior," *Academy of Management Review* 5, no. 2 (June 1980): 281–90.

Fred Luthans and Tim R.V. Davis, "Beyond Modeling: Managing Social Learning Processes in Human Resource Training and Development," *Human Resource Management* (Summer 1981): 19–27.

Tim R.V. Davis and Fred Luthans, "Defining and Researching Leadership as a Behavioral Construct: An Idiographic Approach," *Journal of Applied Behavioral Science* 20, no. 3 (August 1984): 237–51.

Luthans and Robert Kreitner, of Arizona State University, also used social learning theory to expand the operant learning approach to what they call organizational behavior modification, or O.B. Mod. The following works expand on the O.B. Mod. approach, which also is used as a point of departure and perspective, but no data, for *Real Managers*:

Robert Kreitner and Fred Luthans, "A Social Learning Approach to Behavioral Management: Radical Behaviorists 'Mellowing' Out," *Organizational Dynamics* 13, no. 2 (Autumn 1984): 61–75.

Fred Luthans and Robert Kreitner, *Organizational Behavior Modification and Beyond* (Glenview, Ill.: Scott Foresman, 1985).

In addition to the theoretical foundation and perspectives provided by the above references, the present study drew from the following methodological perspectives provided in articles by Luthans and Davis and Luthans and Nancy Morey, of Western Illinois University:

Fred Luthans and Tim R.V. Davis, "An Idiographic Approach to Organizational Behavior Research: The Use of Single Case Experimental Designs and Direct Measures," *Academy of Management Review* 7, no. 3 (July 1982): 380–91.

Nancy Morey and Fred Luthans, "An Emic Perspective and Ethno-science Methods for Organizational Research," *Academy of Management Review* 9, no. 1 (January 1984): 27–36.

Nancy Morey and Fred Luthans, "Refining the Displacement of Culture and the Use of Scenes and Themes in Organizational Studies," *Academy of Management Review* 10, no. 2 (April 1985): 219–29.

The three standardized questionnaries used in the effectiveness analysis reported in Chapter 4 were drawn from:

Paul E. Mott, *The Characteristics of Effective Organizations* (New York: Harper & Row, 1972). (This book contains the questionnaire for organizational effectiveness in terms of the quantity and quality of performance of the work unit.)

Richard T. Mowday, L.W. Porter, and Richard M. Steers, *Employee-Organizational Linkages: The Psychology of Commitment, Absenteeism, and Turnover* (New York: Academic Press, 1982). (This book contains the Organizational Commitment Questionnaire.)

P.C. Smith, L.M. Kendall, and C.L. Hulin, *The Measurement of Satisfaction in Work and Retirement* (Chicago: Rand-McNally, 1969). (This contains the Job Diagnostic Index that measures employee satisfaction.)

The following article by Luthans and Diane Lockwood, of Seattle University, is the most directly related reference to *Real Managers* that describes in detail the derivation of the managerial activities and the reliability and validity analyses: Fred Luthans and Diane Lockwood, "Toward an Observation System for Measuring Leader Behavior in Natural Settings," in *Leaders and Managers: International Perspectives of Managerial Behavior and Leadership*, eds. J. Hunt, D. Hosking, C. Schriesheim, and R. Stewart (New York: Pergamon Press, 1984), 117–41.

The data base for *Real Managers* generated two recent, specialized articles:

Fred Luthans, Stuart Rosenkrantz, and Harry Hennessey, "What Do Successful Managers Really Do? An Observational Study of Managerial Activities," *Journal of Applied Behavioral Science* 21, no. 3 (August 1985): 255–70.

Fred Luthans and Janet K. Larsen, "How Managers Really Communicate," *Human Relations* 39, no. 2 (February 1986): 161–78.

Harry Hennessey is at Florida State University and Janet Larsen is at the University of South Dakota. There are other articles in various stages that draw from the *Real Managers* data base. The interested reader will find details of the samples used, measurement techniques, and statistical analysis in the above articles, especially in the Luthans and Lockwood article.

Besides the above directly related references to the study of *Real Managers,* the text discussion mentioned other authors. Here is a full reference list for the interested reader:

Bass, Bernard M. *Leadership and Performance Beyond Expectations.* New York: Free Press, 1985.

Bolman, L.G. and T.E. Deal. *Modern Approaches to Understanding and Managing Organizations.* San Francisco: Jossey Bass, 1984.

Culbert, S.A. and J.J. McDonough. *Radical Management.* New York: Free Press, 1985.

Fayol, Henri. *General and Industrial Management.* Translated by Constance Storrs. London: Pitman, 1949.

Gulick, Luther. "Notes on the Theory of Organization." In *Papers on the Science of Administration,* edited by Luther Gulick and Lyndall Urwick. New York: Institute of Public Administration, 1937.

Koontz, Harold. "The Management Theory Jungle." *Academy of Management Journal* 4, no. 3 (December 1961): 174–88.

———. "The Management Theory Jungle Revisited." *Academy of Management Review* 5, no. 2 (April 1980): 175–87.

Kotter, John. *The General Managers.* New York: Free Press, 1982.

———. "What Effective General Managers Really Do." *Harvard Business Review* 60, no. 6 (November-December 1982): 156–67.

Likert, Rensis. *The Human Organization.* New York: McGraw-Hill, 1967.

McClelland, David C. *The Achieving Society.* Princeton, N.J.: Van Norstrand, 1961.

———. "The Two Faces of Power." *Journal of International Affairs* 24, no. 1 (1970): pp. 29–47.

Mintzberg, Henry. *The Nature of Managerial Work.* New York: Harper & Row, 1973.

————. "The Manager's Job: Folklore and Fact." *Harvard Business Review* 53, no. 4 (July-August, 1975): 49–61.

Peters, Thomas J. and Robert H. Waterman, Jr. *In Search of Excellence: Lessons from America's Best-Run Companies.* New York: Harper & Row, 1982.

Urwick, Lyndall. *The Elements of Administration.* New York: Harper, 1943.

INDEX

Bass, Bernard M., 182
Bolman, L.G., 182

Career development, 154–155
Carnegie, Dale, 53
Communication activities
  acceptance, 108
  attention, 108
  and body language, 112–113
  communication flows, 96–97
  dealing with barriers to, 112–114
  diagonal, 100–101
  downward, 97–99
  of effective real managers, 67, 68–69
  and empathy, 111–112
  empirical backdrop, 95–96
  examples of, 13–14
  and feedback, 113–115
  flows, 96–102
  importance of, 110–111
  and inference barriers, 104–105
  and language barriers, 105–106
  lateral, 100–101
  and listening skills, 115–116
  of real managers, 107–110
  and simple, repetitive language, 110–111
  of successful real managers, 44–45
  and perceptual barriers, 102–104
  and speaking skills, 116–117
  and status barriers, 106–107
  and understanding, 108
  upward, 99–100
  and writing skills, 116–117
Controlling, 10, 15, 21, 51–52
Culbert, S.A., 182

Davis, Tim R.V., 180
Deal, T.E., 182
Decisionmaking, 11
Delphi process, 9
Disciplining/punishing
  described, 10, 18, 22, 138
  little-by-little strategy, 144–145
  room-for-adjustment strategy, 145–146

Effective real managers
  communication activities of, 68–69

Effective real managers—*continued*
  comparison of successful and,
    161
  defined, 63–66
  determining of, 159–160
  human resource activities of,
    69–71
  myths of, 73–75
  networking activities of, 72
  results of effectiveness analysis,
    66–68
  successful versus, 62–63
  traditional management ac-
    tivities of, 71–72
  traditional profile of, 59–62
  what they do, 160
Exchanging information, 11

Fayol, Henri, 30, 33, 56, 182
Ford, II, Henry, 36

Geneen, Harold, 36
Gulick, Luther, 182

Handling paperwork, 11, 14, 20
Hennessey, Harry, 37, 181, 182
Hosking, D., 181
Hulin, C.L., 181
Human resource management
    activities
  allocating formal rewards and,
    142–143
  conveying appreciation and
    recognition, 140–141
  descriptive categories, 12
  disciplining and punishing, 10,
    18, 22, 138, 144–146
  of effective real managers, 45–
    49
  empirical backdrop, 135–136
  examples of, 18, 22–24, 49–52,
    69–71
  job challenge and, 137–139
  listening to suggestions and,
    139–140
  management of conflict, 146–
    149
  motivation and, 136–143
  performance feedback and,
    141–142
  reinforcement and, 136–143

staffing, 149–150
  of successful real managers,
    69–71
  training and development, 150–
    155
  use of, 67, 68
Hunt, J.G., 11, 179, 181

Iacocca, Lee, 35, 36
Interacting with others, 11

Koontz, Harold, 33, 182
Kotter, John, 7, 26, 36, 182
Kendall, L.M., 181
Kreitner, Robert, 180

Larsen, Janet, K., 98, 181
Larson, Lars L., 179, 182
Likert, Rensis, 45, 182
Lockwood, Diane, 11, 181, 182
Loman, Willy, 53
Luthans, Fred, 11, 37, 98, 179,
    180, 181, 182, 183

McDonough, J.J., 182
Management
  classic, 30–33
  jungle, 33–34
  myths, 27–30, 53–57
  principles of, 31–33
  radical, 163–165
  schools of, 33–34
  transformational, 162–163
Management by walking around,
    90–91
Management jungle, 33–34
Management principles, 31–33
Management skills;
  now and in the future, 173–177
  need for communication skills,
    173–175
  need for interpersonal skills, 175
  for managing stress, 176
  needed in the future, 176–177
  for managing change, 177
Manager success index (MSI), 37
  (see also *Real managers, Ef-
    fective real managers,* and
    Successful real managers)
Managerial activities
  distribution of, 25–26

examples of, 13–24
Kotter study, 7
Mintzberg study, 6–7
observance of, 13–24
relative occurrence of, 24–34
studies of, 6–7
and successful real managers,
    41–43
Managerial effectiveness, 63–66
Managerial myths, 27–30, 53–57,
    73–75
Managerial success analysis,
    36–37
Managing conflict
    described, 11, 18, 23, 183, 146
    cooperation, 147
    cooptation, 174
    third-party negotiators,
        148–149
    use of higher authority, 148
McClelland, David, 54
Mentoring, 128–129, 153
Mintzberg, Henry, 6, 26, 36, 182,
    183
Morey, Nancy, 180, 181
Motivating and reinforcing
    allocating formal rewards,
        142–143
    conveying appreciation and rec-
        ognition, 140–141
    described, 10, 17, 22, 136–143
    increasing job challenge, 137
    listening to suggestions, 139–
        140
    performance feedback, 141–142
Mott, Paul E., 181
Mowday, Richard T., 181

Networking (also see Networking
    activities)
    descriptive categories, 12
    and effective real managers, 72
    examples of, 16–17, 21–22,
        43–44, 72
    and successful real managers,
        38–39
    with outsiders, 16–17, 21
Networking activities
    distribution of, 120
    of effective real managers, 67,
        68, 72

formal, 129–130
impact of, 130–132
importance of, 38–40
and the informal organization,
    121–122
lessons to be learned from,
    132–133
and mentoring, 128–129
and political skills, 127–128
and power, 122–125
and social skills, 125–127
of successful real managers,
    43–44
use of, 41
usefulness of, 129–130

Organizational culture, 166–168
Orientation, 151–152

Peters, Tom, 32, 90, 183
Planning, 10, 15, 50–51, 78–84
Porter, L.W., 181
Power
    as a commodity, 122–123
    use of, 123–125
Principles of management, 31–33

RMs (see Real managers)
Real managers (see also Successful
    real managers and Effective
    real managers)
    activities of, 13–20, 24–27
    background of, 7–13
    communication activities of,
        107–117
    controlling, 10, 21, 51–52
    decisionmaking, 11, 15, 20–21,
        49–50
    disciplining/punishing, 10, 18,
        22
    effective, 3
    exchanging information, 11, 13,
        14, 20
    handling paperwork, 11, 14, 20
    interacting with others, 11, 21
    interviews of, 12–13
    managerial activities of, 41–43
    managing conflict, 11, 18, 23
    motivating/reinforcing, 10, 17,
        22
    myths regarding, 27–30

Real managers—*continued*
planning, 10, 15, 20, 50–51
previous studies, 6–7
results in practice, 26–27
routine communication and, 12, 14, 44–45, 95–117
socializing/politicking, 11, 17, 22
staffing, 10, 19, 23
traditional management, 12, 45–49
training/development, 10, 19, 23–24
Rosenkrantz, Stuart A., 37, 181
Routine communication (see also *Communication activities*)
descriptive categories, 12
examples of, 13–14, 20, 44–45, 68–69
exchanging, 14
paperwork, 20
use of, 41, 66, 68

Schools of management
management process, 33
empirical, 33
human behavior, 33
social system, 33–34
decision theory, 33–34
mathematical, 33–34
Schriesheim, C., 11, 181
Smith, P.C., 181
Socializing/politicking, 11
Staffing
described, 10, 19, 23, 138
developing job descriptions, 149
interviewing job opening candidates, 149–150
the staffing decision, 150
Steers, Richard M., 181
Stewart, R., 11, 181
Successful real managers
activities of, 38–40
analysis by organization and level, 39–40
background on, 36–37
communication activities of, 44–45
comparison of real and, 161
controlling, 51–52
decisionmaking and, 49–50

determination of, 159–160
human resources management activities of, 42, 45–49
importance of networking activities to, 38–39
in perspective, 52
lack of work on, 36
managerial activities and, 41–43
measure of success used, 37
myths of, 53–57
networking activities of, 42, 43–44
planning and, 50–51
traditional management activities of, 42, 49–52
versus effective managers, 62–63
versus least successful, 40–41
what they do, 160

Traditional management activities
activities of effective real managers, 71–72
activities of successful real managers, 49–52
choosing between alternatives, 89–90
controlling, 90–93
coordinating the work, 83–84
cost/benefit analysis, 86–87
decisionmaking, 79, 84–90
defining tasks, 81
descriptive categories, 12
developing efficiency procedures, 87–88
doing preventive maintenance, 92–93
examining the problem, 86
examples of, 15–16, 20–21, 49–52, 71–72
handling operational crises, 88–89
inspecting the work, 90
management by walking around, 90–91
monitoring performance, 91–92
organizing the work, 84
planning, 78–84
scheduling and assigning work, 81–83
setting goals and objectives, 80
use of, 67, 68

Training and development
   career development, 154–155
   described, 10, 19, 23–24, 134
   identifying training needs,
     152–153
   implementation approaches,
     152–153

   and mentoring, 153
   orientation, 151–152

Urwick, Lyndall, 182, 183

Waterman, Jr., Robert H., 90,
   183

ABOUT THE AUTHORS

Fred Luthans is the George Holmes University Distinguished Professor of Management at the University of Nebraska at Lincoln, where he teaches and does research in organizational behavior and management. He served as president of the Academy of Management during 1986. He is a fellow of both the Academy of Management and the Decision Sciences Institute. Professor Luthans has been a visiting scholar at a number of universities and has lectured in the People's Republic of China, the Republic of China, England, Germany, Japan, Korea, Mexico, the Netherlands, and Norway. While serving in the armed forces, he taught at the U.S. Military Academy at West Point. He received his B.A., M.B.A., and Ph.D. degrees from the University of Iowa and did postdoctoral work at Columbia University.

Professor Luthans has published about a dozen books and one hundred articles in applied and academic journals and research reports. The consulting editor for the McGraw-Hill Management Series, he also serves on a number of editorial boards. He is currently an associate editor of *Decision Sciences*. In addition, he is a consultant to both private- and public-sector organizations and conducts workshops on behavioral management in the United States and abroad. His current major work is with Wal-Mart Corporation.

Richard M. Hodgetts is a professor of management at the College of Business at Florida International University in Miami, where he teaches and does research in the general management area. Previously he was a professor of management at the University of Nebraska, Lincoln, and spent a year as a visiting professor at Texas Tech University. Active in the Academy of Management, Professor Hodgetts is a former chair of the Management History Division and was elected a fellow in 1983. He received his bachelor's degree from New York University, his master's from Indiana University, and his doctorate from the University of Oklahoma.

Professor Hodgetts has authored or coauthored fourteen major books and numerous articles. In addition, he authors a weekly business newspaper column entitled "Minding Your Business." He is the president of Hodgetts & Associates, Inc. and is active in training and consulting in industry in the United States and South America. Currently he is engaged in a South American project for an international oil firm and a national government that are seeking assistance in more effectively employing their human resources.

Stuart A. Rosenkrantz is an associate professor of management at Eastern Illinois University. He is also a management consultant and lecturer to many state and private organizations. Previously he served as planning consultant to more than fifty government and corporate organizations. He received his B.G.S., M.S., and Ph.D. degrees from the University of Nebraska.

Professor Rosenkrantz has contributed to several books and published articles in many journals, including the *Journal of Applied Behavioral Science* and *Personnel*. His contributions as an innovator in management, science, and technology have been recognized by the National Defense Science Board and numerous government agencies.